The Growl of Deeper Waters

The Swiss
Selection
of the
International
Poetry Forum

The Growl

of Deeper Waters

Essays by

Denis de Rougemont

Translated from the French by

Samuel Hazo

with Beth Luey

University of Pittsburgh Press

F. Jmm —
Through deep and shallow
waters, yours is the longest
friendship I have.
My best, as always
Sam

PQ 2635
O 9 2 4
D 6 1 3
cop. 2

Library of Congress Cataloging in Publication Data

Rougemont, Denis de, birth date
The growl of deeper waters.

Translation of Doctrine fabuleuse.
"The Swiss selection of the International Poetry
Forum."
  I. Title.
PQ2635.0924D613   841'.9'12   75-33422
ISBN 0-8229-3315-2

All the essays in this book except "Notes on the Unmapped Road" were
first published in French in *Doctrine Fabuleuse*, © 1947, Ides et Calends,
Neuchâtel and Paris.

This book was made possible by a grant from
The Buhl Foundation.

Contents

Preface

Denis de Rougemont's reputation rests securely and superbly on his classical books on love as well as on his vision of Europe. Fewer know him as a master of the short essay or *propos*. When one mentions this genre, one thinks of the essays of Montaigne, Baudelaire's splenetic proems, Alain's or Maurois' provocative tracts on human experience as a whole, Camus' tone poems (there is no other phrase) of the Mediterranean, and Saint-Exupéry's lyrical descriptions of men, machines, and the air.

Denis de Rougemont's concern in the following essays, which, like those of the aforementioned authors, are poetic in conception as well as style, is with the contemporaneity—the timeless contemporaneity—of legend. The original title of the book in French, *Doctrine Fabuleuse*, suggests this, but a literal translation of these words into English is a vapid equivalent, at best. Hence my preference for the more poetic title—*The Growl of Deeper Waters*, which is itself drawn from his essay on Eurydice. This suggests to me how de Rougemont has attempted to see the doctrine within or beneath the fable and how, in each of his essays, he has managed to convey the growl of these deeper waters to the reader. I can only hope that Beth Luey and I have been faithful to the spirit of his insights. In this regard I would be remiss if I did not acknowledge my debt to Svetlana Kluge Harris, Odile Postic, and Robert Cook for their help in transliterating various parts of the text, to Denis de Rougemont himself for his final suggestions, and to The Buhl Foundation and its Director, David Henderson, for a grant that made the entire project possible.

SAMUEL HAZO, *Director*
International Poetry Forum

ix

Orientation

Myths narrate reality as a continuous event. Mythological fables glorify the daily drama of affective and spiritual life, that is, human life, just as the equations of physics translate the forms of energy into something that we consider objective. These two approaches to reality, the dramatic and the statistical, seem to me equally valid. But the statistical may some day become a special case of the dramatic.

True myths are universal. The story of Cendrillon can be found among the most diverse peoples of all ages. (One hundred and thirty-one versions of it have been collected.) These people never communicated with one another; they communicated only with the constitutive reality of our human condition, the vast treasure of dynamic forms from which arise, at certain decisive moments, the archetypes of our most sincere and startling emotions.

Finally, myths reveal the common themes of situations which appear very different. Thus, one comes across Don Juan amid the thought of Nietzsche, or the torment of Tantalus in a story by Jean-Paul.* In the same way, we apply sayings and proverbs to various occasions of everyday life, which can be identified by this popular algebra. Likewise, preachers restore the relevance of the day's Gospel lesson in a way that is mythological in the sense in which I am using the word here.

It seems to me that the merging of these three words— myth, event, reality—was by nature a better way of guiding the reader than an apparently methodical discourse which, at the beginning of this work on the fabulous, would have been wrong because it was not itself fabulous.

DENIS DE ROUGEMONT

The Growl of Deeper Waters

First Postcard Dialogue

Of Rain and Sunshine

Lord Arthur. I would like to ask you a question, Sonnette. A rather serious question which amounts to asking whether you are capable of love or are simply adorable. Here it is: Do you prefer a rainy day or good weather?

Sonnette. You're funny. I'm the one who makes the day rainy or sunny!

Lord Arthur. That would surely be a wise answer if only you knew what you were talking about. But really, what do sunshine and rain mean to you? Are they laughing and crying, happiness and sadness? Do you prefer one to the other?

Sonnette. Since you're an utter pedant, within five minutes I won't be able to tell whether the day is good or bad.

Lord Arthur. I seriously think you never knew, any more than you ever knew whether you preferred happiness to sadness. You don't know where your real good lies. That is why these words seem simple, obvious, and inconsequential to you. You admit that "fine" weather is the opposite of "bad" weather, but you have never tried to find out what "fine" weather really means or whether storms can be "beautiful." And you still think that happiness can exist outside our pain, or even that it is the opposite of pain, little girl! Your dreams always conjure up the same picture postcard, the inevitable ideal of those who have no opinion on good weather. Listen to me, Sonnette. Your actions, your thoughts, your ideas about love actually come from picture postcards, not from reality. You don't like to think about pain. (*Silence.*) No doubt, Sonnette, you wear short patent leather boots when it rains?

Sonnette. When I was a little girl, I used to like to walk barelegged in the rain along the edge of the forest. The grass was full of slugs and little snails, and the wet raspberries had a delicious, funny taste. I used to come home very proud that my knees were scratched like the boys'. At night, when someone invariably wished that it would be nice the next day, I thought to myself that I liked the grass better when it was wet.

3

Lord Arthur. It's often said that women are by nature pagan. But pagans are always religious, whereas women today are just cunning.

Sonnette. Lord Arthur, you really amuse me. You must be jealous tonight. Whenever you give in to your mania for raking up metaphysical theories about nothing, it's because of some amorous spite. If I provoke you a little more, you'll end up proving that one has to be a Christian to speak wisely about rain or fine weather.

Lord Arthur. I always considered you extremely intelligent, and I'm deeply disappointed that you have no more sense than a bird. Sonnette, if you were a pagan or a Christian, you would know what fine weather is. If you were a pagan and worshiped the light, fine weather would be a god made visible, and "happiness" would be the name for his presence. But one day, the light died around us. It died on the surface of things to be reborn within man. And since that moment, none of the events that take place around us is important, except the one that occurs at the same time within an individual. Thus everything is changed, but few realize it. Few know the path which leads from sign to reality, the way of incarnation.

Long spring rainfalls on the quiet countryside, storms in the high hills—that is my beautiful weather—for me, the climate of presence. For that "good," I love these rainy days. I know that at dawn and at other times, I have possessed it. Now, I no longer have to choose among many created objects, but only to find the meaning that suits me. And when I know where these things belong, there I house my thoughts.

Fable tells us that *Myscellus, citizen of Argos, did so. Unable to unravel the meaning of the oracle which told him to build a city where he found rain and fine weather, he met a courtesan in Italy who was crying, and there he built Crotona.*

Sonnette. Tell me, Lord Arthur, if I were crying, how would the weather be for you?

Lord Arthur. . . . that beautiful word: courtesan. Perhaps it's not her beauty, but her tears that arouse me. Because there she stands, wrapped in her sin—like a courtesan. But you are just a little girl.

Second Postcard Dialogue

Physical Beauty

The painter. (*Laughing.*) . . . and he said, straightening his glasses like an art critic, "No wonder your Leda is reduced to being loved by a swan. What man would want such a woman?"
The husband. And you answered?
The painter. I told him that my swan didn't need glasses.
The husband. You could have pointed out that your Leda truly exists only for and with the swan. An art critic should understand that. . . . What was charming Ellen saying?
The painter. As you say, Leda is a woman-with-a-swan. She is made for him. I would not say the same of Ellen. She's certainly not made for a critic! Pretty, yes. But I thought, seeing them together, that my Leda is much more "moral" when she kisses her swan than many women are when they kiss their lawful, monstrous husbands! It's a matter of propriety, as we were saying yesterday.* I find their union disagreeable.
The husband. You are making the same mistake as he, only in the other direction.
The painter. What you you mean?
The husband. He was wrong to speak of your Leda as if she were not in a frame, and you are just as wrong to speak of this couple as if they were a painting.
The painter. Well! Should I conclude that there is one morality within a frame and another morality outside the frame, which would apply, for example, to this critic and his wife? That is a distinction I did not expect from you.
The husband. The distinction is not in *my* mind, but in yours. If there is such a thing as a natural ethic—or aesthetic—I suppose that its principle is unique, but it contains all the world's diversity. For this ethic concerns each individual's *way of life*, not his classification; carnal man, not conceptual man.
The painter. Excuse me, but I only understand what I see, and I don't see clearly what you have just said. A unique principle . . . which concerns . . . ? Help me.
The husband. An ethic which concerns each man's con-

crete, private way of life, an ethic not only which takes into account this way of life, but whose only principle is to ensure it—or rather to ensure its continuing risk. But many things would have to be explained.

The painter. Wait! Let's go back to Leda. I'm trying to see. According to you, what is her concrete, private, way of life? What is her risk?

The husband. You answered the first question yourself. Leda is made for the swan; she exists only in relation to him. That is her entire ethic, aesthetic, and existence. She is in the picture; she cannot leave it; she cannot untangle herself from the opulent embrace I was admiring before. Anyone who wants to judge her as a woman, and not as Leda, as *this* Leda, is judging her in a void, speaking empty words, and acting like a moralist— not like a man of feeling. On the other hand, anyone who regards her within her own existence, in her relationship with the swan and within that frame, also regards her according to her own risk, and can therefore judge her.

The painter. Judge her! That's all well and good, but if the aesthetic and the ethic are the one and only reality, I know what that means!

The husband. Go on.

The painter. You are going to tyrannize the art of painting in the name of your dogmas, to manufacture allegory or the Bergsonism of the Prix de Rome, a pictorial metaphysics and a metaphysical pictoriality! I call that academicism. Ideal beauty and moral good are laughable. They don't correspond to any known color. I am interested in the interplay of tones and masses, come what may, and you can judge it as you like. What matters to me is to make values and lines move. I see only one risk here: Will it or won't it sell? This risk comes from the stupidity of the public, so it's not an aesthetic question.

The husband. All right, calm down. We agree. If you'll listen to me, there will be no further misunderstanding. Your colors exist in their relationship on a canvas; that is their ethic and their risk. You exist in relation to the picture you are painting. That is your ethic as a painter, and it is also the place of your risk, the place where you create your own standards, where you are both creator and judge, where you are your own truth, *index sui et falsi.* Thus you exist truly, and you are not subject to any rule outside your action.

Furthermore, the art lover, before your painting, far from judging it according to some canon, must discover the peculiar relationships which reveal the inner law of this painting. He must first submit to the painting's own life in order to let it affect him, to let it enter him in a living, unpredictable way. Of course, this relationship is also a risk. Then, but only then, judgment can intervene. Is this a moral or an aesthetic judgment? It is real. It intervenes by virtue of a *reality* which is neither in the painting, nor in my eyes, nor even exactly in their encounter. I will say "beautiful" if this encounter evokes the reality in question, directs me toward it, points it out to me. I will judge as "ugly" whatever distracts me or makes me doubt its existence and proximity.

If you follow my argument, you must see that this reality is not some sort of academic model or universal canon.

The painter. I see that it's not a postcard. For me, as I told you, anything academic is more or less a postcard. Take yesterday's critic. You needn't scrape much to find the postcard in the back of his mind.

The husband. I am going to surprise you.

The painter. Try.

The husband. Like a magician, I am going to pull a magnificent postcard out of your head!

The painter. I'm counting. One, two, . . .

The husband. Three! Why do you say of a woman: "She is pretty"? Of a woman like Ellen, for example, who doesn't belong to you in any way?

The painter. (*After thinking a moment.*) It's hard to say. Don't you think that everyone has his "type"? his "type of woman"? It's the painters who create these types. Rubens or Renoir, Ingres, and goodness knows who else. My Leda . . .

The husband. You're not going to get off that easily. Maybe Rubens or Renoir illustrated your postcards, or maybe you painted them yourself, but they are nonetheless postcards, picture postcards. And you are judging Renoir about the same way your barber judges one of those cards with a wax-complexioned lover leaning over a bluish beauty, all on an artistic, sepia background. I am speaking, of course, of disinterested judgments. When it comes to making love, or simply making portraits, I like to think that you use a more genuine standard. But you probably would not be able to define it.

The painter. Perhaps I haven't any "genuine standard."

The husband. There are men who believe they have no ethics, no philosophy, no religion, and who even explain why! I am going to tell you how they live: in shame and depression, if they have any character. If they have none, they live in constant confusion and in the degradation of all their prejudices. Beauty, for example. Physical beauty exists only within a true relationship, and that is precisely what they don't know. Physical beauty is the view one has of a certain relationship between a subject and an object, between a man and a woman, for example. If the subject has nothing more in mind than a postcard, he does not know himself as a subject. He thinks that beauty is indeed *in* the body that he is contemplating, a body which offers or denies him certain traits conforming to his ideal. But again, he is not aware of projecting this ideal onto objects. He says only that he never finds a real woman who is perfectly beautiful or exactly embodies his type. It is a torture which is too seldom mentioned, this torture endured by postcard men. It is unconscious, of course, but effective. In strong souls, it produces endless flight, the anxious curiosity called instability—a Don Juan.

9

For most people, it ends in submissiveness. The subject surrenders and gradually molds himself to the object he chose by chance, necessity, or conjecture. He blurs his postcard. Finally, he thinks he is fulfilled because he has no further needs.

The painter. Who has no postcard in his mind? Or even better, what difference is there between a man who has never had a postcard in his mind and a man who has lost his mental postcard because he has blurred it completely and has accepted what he has?

The husband. I'll answer you without hesitation. The only man who has no postcard in the back of his mind is the one who, when he is with a woman, not only scorns the idea of judging her beautiful or ugly, who not only stands silent, but remains silent until he understands and evaluates the true meaning of his uneasiness.

The painter. And then?

The husband. Then he remains silent or else he knows he is in love.

You will probably ask what the others do, those who have renounced the ideal, who no longer believe in it—or rather think they no longer believe in it, because they have given it up for themselves. Of course, they behave absurdly. How could it be otherwise? They persist in passing judgment on all women, on all *other* women, according to popular aesthetic canons, or current academic prejudices, or on the basis of that statistical species composed of the race's most striking features—democratic beauty *par excellence*, ugliness itself. You can't tell Mr. Smith, whose obese wife has been cosmetically rejuvenated, that the ideal does not exist, that the ideal of beauty is a farce, that beauty is not an image but an act, a spiritual act. And you can't even say this to console his neighbor, Simpson, who can't afford surgery to reduce his wife's oversized bosom. You would be denounced. People would smile spitefully when you entered the room. They might even suspect you of sadism or of perpetrating some hideous plan for social subversion.

The painter.   And they would be right. You see, these people would never get angry if they took beauty seriously, as my profession requires. If they get angry, and if they lose their heads each time you appear, it is because they don't know what you're talking about. The city dweller is like that. Everything he does not understand seems to be a sneak attack on his position. But it's too easy to make fun of these people. It's degrading—like tilting at windmills. I know a much more interesting—possibly unique—case: yours. You defend your theories on the relativity of physical beauty and at the same time are married to a beautiful woman, if I may say so.

The husband.   You may not. No one may! My wife is not beautiful! She is not ugly! She is not indifferent! I simply cannot stand your saying anything at all about her beauty. I repeat: Beauty is not an image or a comparison of images. It is an act of the mind—a completely personal act. There is no beauty without context, without a relationship between an *I* and a *you*, face to face. If you do not understand, I will have to consider *you* dangerous, mad, and shameless. For you do not give up easily. You are a modern man. For you, fences are made to be jumped.

The painter.   And your theories are made to render life impossible!

The husband.   Perhaps that proves they are true, that they make greatness possible, whereas our lives are mere confusion.

What is this nonsense of separating a husband and wife? What gives you the right to judge one of us as if she did not combine with the other as "one flesh"? Or are you going to claim that the beauty of a couple is simply the sum of the two beauties united in it? That would be nonsense. No, the beauty of a couple is an act, like marriage. It is completely different from the beauty of the man alone and of the woman alone; it annihilates these beauties and supersedes them once and for all. If you take marriage seriously, as I profess to do, you can no longer speak of a husband and wife as two bachelors placed arbitrarily side by side. But that is what you have just done. You should know that I don't consider my wife beautiful. She does not correspond at all with the "ideal" I had in mind when I met her. But there is something between us, something real and unique. When I look at my wife and love her—when I understand her essence and existence—I am completely directed toward a deeper, freer reality, more dangerous, simpler, more urgent, more real. This beauty is not in my wife's face; yet, without her face, I could not imagine it. This beauty is not in me; yet, if I were different, it would not exist for me. It transcends us; yet it depends on us. It is entirely *different* from what we are together; but we can only reach it together. It is not our union; but only our union shows it to us, points it out as something beyond itself, and directs us to its reality. If this were not so, would we truly be married?

Third Postcard Dialogue

The Incognito Hero

The Advertising Agent. Sir, you undoubtedly know the series of color portraits published by the major magazines, *"L'Homme Distingué,"* "The Man of Distinction." I have come to ask the honor of taking your picture for this series.

X (A celebrity of the day). I suppose I would have to sit in an armchair, cross my legs, look at the camera, and hold a tall glass of whiskey.

The Agent. Exactly. Permit me.... These six bottles are a gift from our firm. We have wanted to meet you for a long time, and only the numerous trips required by your career . . .

X. Do sit down, please, and let's talk. What do you mean by a man of distinction?

The Agent. Here is the list of those who have consented to pose for us. A glance will assure you that you are in good company.

X. Then you publish these portraits to advertise your whiskey? Good. The general idea seems simple. You induce the reader to think: "If Mr. X, a man of distinction, drinks this whiskey, I will become distinguished by drinking it." Emulate the man of distinction, and you will distinguish yourself. Well, in my opinion, this short sentence contains a contradiction in terms. How can you distinguish yourself by imitating? How can you become different by struggling to be the same? Suppose your effort succeeds and everyone adopts your brand. It will cease to be a mark of distinction. You will be lost.

The Agent. Not at all. Should this blessed day ever come, we will simply change our slogan. Instead of saying: "Be distinguished, drink 'Nelson,'" we will say, "Do as everyone does, drink 'Nelson.'" Such is our craft, and I am sure I can use it to your benefit, whether you like it or not.

X. And so your men of distinction will have become men of vulgarity, picture postcards that are the very model of the commonplace. Do you see the risk I am taking?

The Agent. All those in prominent positions have taken

the risk cheerfully so far, and anyway, the danger is not great. Take the old Austrian emperor, Franz-Joseph. All the coachmen in the film versions of Viennese operettas used to imitate his appearance and wear the same sideburns. That didn't prevent him from remaining emperor and a thoroughly distinguished man.

X. In fact, he was said to be very polite. Politeness is the only quality I know which makes a man distinguished and at the same time exactly like an accepted model. And even then, I am not sure about the second point. Conforming to good models comes from correctness, but true courtesy is born of ingenuity and especially courage, whose first level is self-control. In short, it is the beginning of heroism. By the way, in your gallery of men of distinction, have you included any heroes?

The Agent. We are proud to have taken the portraits of Admiral Grandisson and General MacAlfred. But since we live in a democratic country, we have also taken a few well-decorated GIs.

X. Those were published during the war, I assume?

The Agent. Of course. Since the war, we have turned to athletes, movie stars, and businessmen.

X. In other words, to those who can be imitated. During the war, the public was won over to heroism. Heroism was even made compulsory for millions of our contemporaries. But that was another contradiction. A hero is a man of great courage, but the *greatest* courage ceases the moment it is officially prescribed. And I'll add that it is rarely popular. Perhaps I must go further and say that its very nature is to be unpopular—or even never to be seen. It is always unique and unequaled, its motivations unknown, because it is produced at the very moment when a man is deprived of reassuring patterns. He is cast before an unprecedented fate to which he would undoubtedly give way if he were to resort to a known example, no matter how great.

The Agent. I can see that you are a lover of paradoxes. Who, in your opinion, is the hero of our time?

X. Someone, sir, whose portrait you will never take. I dare say you would never even think of it, because our age knows only the "best-in-class." The real hero would be inimitable, beyond classification, without precedent and without successors, taking a risk that he alone established, assuming it and conquering it without showing any effort, relying only on his own energy. If he exists, he resembles nothing. He is invisible as a person, unnoticed as an individual. Perhaps he even goes about in disguise, in the sense that he is noted for a certain feature which is really not representative and which diverts attention. He may be someone who has *not* performed a certain action that would have made him famous, rich, or powerful in the eyes of the world and who *did not do it* because of a vocation that his faith alone could understand. And yet *everything* tempted him—reason, morality, and the good of his people.

The Agent. I would call someone like that a failure or a victim of pride who refuses to play his social role. If the hero is not glorious, who will be? The expectations of the masses will be betrayed, and we know that they need someone to admire. But now it's my turn to point out a contradiction in terms when you speak of an "unknown hero."

X. I was waiting for you to say that. All things being equal, let's take two physicists. They have both discovered, on the same day, the secret of the atomic bomb. One refuses to develop it, burns his papers, and quietly goes off to play a game of pool. The second grabs his chance for glory and becomes a national hero; you recently published his picture. Note that the first one remains unknown, and this is precisely what makes him the true hero. And I would add that it is he who probably has best fulfilled his social role.

The Agent. You have to admit that your concept of a hero

totally lacks sex appeal! Moreover, if your ideal is really the person you have just described, whom I would simply call "The Unrecognized," you must be rather unhappy.

X.   Too simplistic an attack. My point still stands. Any well-known man will tell you that he considers his true purpose un-recognized, at least if he isn't vulgar and doesn't take pride in the usurped glory that publicity has forced upon him. But let's leave these scruples aside. The main difference between the man you will seek out because he is proclaimed eminent and the hero whom no one can see for the reasons I just mentioned, is that the former believes in luck and happiness, while the latter believes in salvation.

The Agent.   Here again, I don't see any distinction or serious difficulty. If I were a philosopher or a priest, I would try to convince the public that true happiness lies in salvation. That would do the trick.

X.   But those who believed you might be lost; in any case they would be tricked.

I see that you still don't understand me. Let me give you another example. You've heard of Kierkegaard, that Danish philosopher whom all your magazines feel obliged to mention or even discuss. The other day one of them asked me for Kierkegaard's address. It gave me pleasure to provide it. It's a flat stone in a Danish cemetery. This man believed not in happiness, but in salvation. He believed not in the masses, but in personal courage. Nor did he believe that such courage could be taught to the masses by the press, radio, and advertising so that some personal courage could finally be obtained *en masse* or that one could mix all sorts of things with impunity. You see, Kierkegaard was the perfect type of the maladjusted man, the social outcast, the "lascivious viper," the rebel who refuses to understand, and the unrepentant negativist who sits in his corner passionately saying no. He was so "distinguished" that some say he died of it. So you can no longer interview him, and that is his good luck. For, if I know you, you wouldn't have been happy until you had dragged him in front of a microphone to explain his great idea to the masses—the idea that nothing important can be told to the masses. And this recluse's radio program would be heard every Sunday by forty million people eager to outdo their neighbors. Imagine this last cry of desperate irony: "Do as I do! Be the exception!"

The Agent. What a marvelous idea for an article! I think the picture of you will be good. We took it while you were speaking on your favorite subject. You were animated, dynamic, completely *à l'aise*—it will be perfect!

X. (*Seized by a sudden rage, he grabs a bottle of whiskey and smashes the camera.*)

The Agent. Sir, I tip my hat to you! I bet this gesture will give you as much publicity as the full-page color photo we will take some other time. (*He is about to leave.*) Wait a minute, I think I have my title: "The Incognito Hero!"

X. (*He tries to seize a second bottle, but the agent is already gone. All that is left for him is to drink in order to forget.*)

Fourth Postcard Dialogue

Ars Prophetica, or *Of a Language Which Refuses to Be Clear*

The Critic. I have read your three postcard dialogues, and I like them.... Well, I don't exactly *like* them. They irritate and annoy me. But I can't forget them.

The Author. Nothing is more reliable than the memory of offenses. I sometimes feel that there is no praise I would prefer to being reproached for my writings. I would like to see that as proof that they are "serious" in the same sense that a wound is serious.

The Critic. Yes, yes. But don't try to prove it by exaggerating my criticism. What bothered me, I believe, was that in my opinion you are still not clear enough.

The Author. And why be clear, may I ask? You are not going to tell me that this is the proper way to make oneself understood?

The Critic. One would want to be sure that you understand yourself sufficiently.

The Author. Sufficiently for what?

The Critic. Sufficiently not to be duped by your own sentences. Writing, especially in French, is not the same as playing a violin. All of a sudden you play a double stop, the passages can't be distinguished, and you change key. It would be nice to know that you realize you have done so. It seems to me that you are not ruthless toward your own ideas. They seduce you from afar, and when you present them to us, they already have your complicity and a certain premature passion that takes us by surprise.

The Author. Isn't this always the case? I mean, isn't every writer first seduced, or on the contrary offended, by his images or ideas, before he can avow any reason?

The Critic. Indeed, but you must compose introductions. You must persuade us that your tastes are indeed reasons, and that these reasons are ours. Either you write poetry and play on the element of surprise, or else you speak of ideas. In that case, we must think at each moment: "I was going to say that!"

But don't mix the two or you will be suspected of cheating.

The Author. Shall we talk about clarity? I can tell that this will lead us back to the subject of my two preceding dialogues.

The Critic. Will you at least be on your guard against your own obscurity?

The Author. It is this very bias toward clarity which I would like to submit to your suspicions. If you permit me, I will be so ridiculous as to defend my own point of view. This blunder may teach me more than an obliging artifice. In any case, this is all between us, and you will not take advantage of my confessions. Anyway, they will probably be exaggerated.

The Critic. So many precautions! You are like that hero in God knows which of Toepffer's sketchbooks who pretends to pretend in order better to conceal. What is clarity, in your opinion?

The Author. As soon as you ask this question, you are bound to get either insipid or mysterious answers. Couldn't it be that clarity is nothing but a linguistic convention, a tribal password, or a sort of style backed up by usage?

The Critic. Now what? You know that any language is a system of conventions!

The Author. Our ordinary language undoubtedly is, and even more strictly our intellectual and scientific language, which differs from ordinary language in its effort to register its conventions. But these are not the only possible means of expression.

The Critic. I was hoping that you would choose between a strictly poetic language and the "clear and distinct" language that belongs to the contest of ideas.

The Author. That belongs to the contest of clear ideas! But we must first agree on the necessity of such clarity. I cannot conceive or respect any general necessity other than that imposed by the *purpose* of a thought.

The Critic. Let's stay, if you don't mind, at the level of language. Isn't the coherence of arguments together with the precise fitting of these arguments to reality the goal of expression?

The Author. Yes, in a Cartesian world, the world of discourse. Because the *Discourse on Method* defines only one method of discourse. The final goal of discourse is nothing but coherence, with truth itself regulated to the logic of a succession of sentences. In other words, Cartesian discourse has no transcendent goal. It starts from what it assumes to be clear and distinct, and moves by deduction. The convention of such a language is that everything is given at the start, and the point is not to introduce into the chain of reasoning anything which has not already been measured, enumerated, and defined in simple terms. It is my turn to distrust such an advantageous convention.

The Critic. It seems to me that one must recognize it as a guarantee against the illusions of flashy rhetoric. Romanticism might lose patience with such a scrupulous pace, but that is because it wants to be deceived and to deceive.

The Author. As far as I am concerned, I fear a less naive deceit in Cartesian simplicity. After all, where in the world can you find anything "clear, distinct, and easy to understand" it itself? Isn't the world in which we live and speak, as some Russian called it, "the world of the inaccurate and the unresolved"? or, as Descartes himself wrote, the world of "badly compassed" things? Doesn't the application of unprejudiced reason to the world as it is have the immediate effect of multiplying mystery and logical absurdity? Look at Kafka. . . . I ask myself whether Cartesianism hasn't duped us once and for all, from the start, by decreeing—in whose name, I ask you?—the clarity and simplicity of certain abstract postulates. My distrust comes from the ulterior motive which governed the choice of these so-called primary data. It isn't entirely correct to resort to the term "ulterior motive." One should rather say "ulterior image."

The Critic. Would it be too Cartesian to ask you to clarify that?

The Author. I shall try to do it with an example. The method created by Descartes has become the method of science. It is the one our physicists, chemists, and mathematicians use to formulate what they call laws. Fine. But how do they obtain those formulas? Let us say by examining the numbers which sum up their experiments. I don't believe any of it. Open a scientific volume. At the end of each abstract you will find several *sentences* interpreting the results. Now the scientist has chosen these sentences to meet two requirements: On the one hand, they must allow transition, via some sort of abstract symbolism—if I may say so—to a mathematical formula. On the other hand—and this is what is important—it is assumed that they correspond to the language of common sense, to the images that the phenomenon would form to a nonscientific observer.

Now, these sentences together form a coherent discourse on the properties of matter. And this discourse is only *a certain system of images.* If it is different from ordinary language, it is primarily because of this coherence, that is, because of this determination to exclude the ordinarily contradictory meanings of words. Accordingly, the laws formulated by science, these models of clear expression, in fact rely on ordinary forms of the language with their special shades of meaning removed.

This process is harmless as long as it is used by scientists, since legitimate science is only *one* way to speak about reality and is constantly being corrected by facts. But I cry treachery when the philosopher or essayist, seduced by axiomatic clarity, claims to *start out* from elementary truths which are nothing but abstractions drawn from our linguistic forms. I would like to phrase this more simply. The treachery of a clear deduction consists in its pretending to start from a limited number of recognized facts while the whole and the end escape us! As if it were permissible, or even possible, to start with certain elements and declare them *known* when one methodically ignores the whole on which they depend and which is their only basis.

The Critic. I would follow you better if you could show me an example of Descartes' resorting to these ordinary language forms.

The Author. Let us take the third rule of his method: "To carry on my reflections in due order, commencing with objects that were the most simple and easy to understand." This seems clear—I mean, in accordance with common sense. However, I detect behind this judgment the strangest illusion of the intellect. It is a popular maxim. It is accepted as so obvious that citing it in a discussion is almost insolent. This maxim confirms the general necessity to "begin at the beginning." Descartes, who has just, without wincing, likened an object's simplicity to the ease of knowing it—again a linguistic trick—is not going to back away from another feat: to lay down that the simplest is also the closest and that one must begin there. This is undoubtedly the nastiest trick every played on writers of ideas! To begin at the beginning! To proceed from the simple to the complex! It seems so sensible! The beautiful cliché, the pretty absurdity, the magnificent postcard! If human experience has established one thing—I would say for once and for all—it is that one must always start at the end, with the total vision, with the revelation of ultimate ends. One can only grasp the parts from the whole, and not the other way around.

The Critic. I notice once more with some curiosity the way your remarks slide around. You are going to switch without warning to theological propositions. Let me confess my incompetence and watch without interrupting further the development of thoughts which are strangely foreign to me. You were talking about a total vision?

The Author. Does this expression seem senseless to you? Consider once and for all how totally I lack reason. Let me speak my eschatological jargon freely.

I was saying that the Cartesian deduction works on postcards. It arranges its marks in an orderly fashion and then takes off backward toward the unknown, its eyes glued to its own strategy. From then on one imagines its moving with so many precautions, checking each step along the way, that it doesn't know its goal and would even consider the belief that this goal exists an annoying obstacle.

For me, it's almost the opposite. I know that I am in the dark. I can only walk in confusion. But if I walk at all, it is because I have seen the goal at certain moments. I *believe* I have seen it. It is an illuminating, instantaneous vision whose trace quickly vanishes before my eyes. But it is enough to guide a few steps. I risk the other steps in the dark, in the night of faith or presentiment, sustained by the hope of a renewed vision. This is the direction, the orientation of my method, and that is why I told you that one can only understand it by starting at the end. It is only right that it seems absurd to the rational observer.

The Critic. The peculiarity of such a vision is, I suppose, that it cannot be communicated?

The Author. It would be better to say that it cannot be described. This is related to its very reality, to its instantaneous fullness, which discourages analysis. You can't give the sensation of whiteness by describing the seven colors. That is why the language of vision or of faith, were it pure, would be absolutely inexplicable—and obvious. One would merely have to reflect endlessly on the form that symbolizes the whole and all of its parts. Of course, I cannot produce any example of such perfection. But these limits had to be indicated to clarify precisely everything in between, in the twilight of this debate.

I now see two sorts of language. To keep it simple, let's recall the two means of expression, equally rigorous but mutually exclusive. The first would be scientific law. Its conventions are clarity and absence of contradiction. The second would be the one whose limits I was trying to suggest in speaking of a language that is inexplicable and yet obvious. The verb "imply" might best distinguish this type from the former, whose function is apparently to explain.

Yes, this contrast is going to help us: To imply the real as such, without explaining certain ways of reducing it to the requirements of a coherent discourse, is without doubt the role of the language of parable. And that is what causes its obscurity. To speak in parables is to attempt to express facts or ideas by considering the whole that comprises them. Or it is to be wary of defining them apart from that ultimate end toward which one strains. Cartesian or scientific language tries to reduce facts or ideas to a few isolated elements. It naturally takes the shape of a discourse, of sentences tied together by inference. But if I speak in parables, I only worry about a certain orientation. And it is by beginning at the end, once again, that the contradictions become clear and are resolved, and not by beginning with elements that I would have distinguished from the beginning. A parable can be understood by its ending, just like Columbus' departing to discover a visionary America. And this end, this term, this *telos*, all the hiatuses, all the obscurities, all the paralogisms of language must show that this end is beyond them, which arguments based on deduction cannot do. That is why the discourse of a prophet is the opposite of a scientific discourse. The event alone gives it its sense. The parable is therefore an enigma whose meaning lies in its vision.

The Critic. How do you explain my pleasure in reading certain parables whose eschatological meaning, I am sure, escapes me completely?

The Author. One day I asked a little girl why Jesus always spoke in parables to his disciples, knowing that they would not understand. Here is what she told me: Jesus told stories so the disciples would remember them better later on. It's like nuts with very hard shells. You can take them along and know they will not spoil, and open them when you are hungry.

The Critic. Still one small question, if you don't mind. Who has the right to speak in parables and to be obscure, like the prophets?

The Author. The right? No one, of course! No one has any such right, if by "right" you mean the formal guarantee of custom. But it often happens that one forgets the great and serious reasons for remaining silent, or for speaking only according to right and decency and in very clear terms. It happens that certain madmen, ecstatics, or profligate souls submit to the hazards of flattering delusions. They call that poetry.

One can, however, imagine another attitude such that the question of right would no longer be raised. It is the attitude of the man who has seen something, or simply believes he has seen it, and who would like to rediscover his vision and have other men see it. Visions, unlike postcards, don't transmit themselves. It is therefore necessary to point the mind in a certain direction by means of words and sentences which can, ironically, be understood in themselves and in their literal meaning, but whose ultimate meaning can be perceived only as a vision—any kind of vision. I say that the man who has *seen* something must speak the language of the prophets and compose parables. If his prophecies are disappointing and his parables barren, he is nevertheless a prophet. But he will be judged by his end.

You will admit that under these conditions it takes a very special type of naiveté to burden oneself with the risk of being obscure. It was good enough for the man from Patmos who had seen the end of history. The magnitude of his vision saved him. But there are less glorious visions which do not embrace the world from top to bottom in a stroke of lightning. I refer to those furtive visions which compared to the vision of the apostles are what the microcosm is to the macrocosm—signs of the Whole and of the End, but only signs, summaries, partial but significant captives. Of course, whoever could fix them in place would rediscover the Apocalypse, just as Cuvier rediscovered prehistory starting from an isolated vertebra. But forgetting comes with the first doubt.

The small visions of men of little faith, visions of the end of our brief passions—wealth, beauty, power—that's all it takes to reduce us to prophetic language. It is the same risk, but not the same grandeur. The great prophets, "Judah's sentries," were justified in their delirium, but a prophet of earthly things, a prophet without a divine mission, what sort of defense will he dare bring forth which will not also be his own Judgment?

Mirrors

or *How One Loses Eurydice and Himself*

Stephen is a faddist, like all young people of his generation. But his mania has nothing to do with cars. He is rather interested in various types of human beings. He receives little gratitude for his curiosity. This wouldn't matter if his curiosity didn't disappoint him. He is, no doubt, too impatient, asking more of human beings than they can give. In any case, they owe him nothing, do they?

But he does not agree. He is not content to wait like a good boy for the world, in its own good time, to give him his small share. He has been told that he has to deserve this small share and try to become somebody. But that only leaves him to recoil into himself. "He goes back to himself, unable to get anything to hold to," as one of our classics says.*

Rejected by the world because he is not yet somebody, Stephen tries to find out what he can be. This is another mania of his generation. But here again he distinguishes himself. He does not write books to pursue a *me* which always pretends to hide behind the next page, leading the reader down the primrose path to the last page—where he announces coldly that he does not exist. No. He has noticed that these times can be defined by an abundance of autobiographies, as well as mirrors. That is why he installs a mirror on his work table, where he can surprise himself at any moment.

This exercise (try it) soon becomes an obsession. Stephen spends hours at a time staring himself in the eye. He varies the play of light and emotion on his face. He discovers a sort of laugh at the corners of his mouth in moments of intense dejection and many more inconsistencies of this sort, which intrigue him no end. Even when he is very tired, he wants to see the fatigue in his eyes. Dwelling on himself, he becomes lost in Eleatic meditations. Sleep delivers him. In the morning he runs to look at himself. He is ugly. Cowardly, he pities himself. These sessions hurt him, debilitate him; but admitting this only ties him more secretly to his adventure.

We live in a flamboyant decor of mirrors. At each step Stephen meets his head, his full portrait. He sees himself shaving and taking a bath; his reflection descends before him in the elevator mirror, follows him along the sidewalks; he catches it between shoes, tags, and dolls; it precedes him into restaurants, flouts him briefly when cars pass, and ridicules him at the barber's.

Now it is with a sort of anguish that he looks for it. He wants to see himself as he appears to others. But when, by chance, he sees his image like that of any passerby, he immediately feels alienated from himself and so profoundly different from his appearance that he doubts his reality.

The mystery of seeing his own eyes frightens him. He searches them for a revelation and finds only the desire for a revelation.

Can one be hypnotized by one's own gaze? Only that chant to himself could give him back the certainty of being. But he exhausts himself in a perspective of giddily diminishing reflections which lead him astray in his own night. I will skip a few deliriums and a number of superstitions.

Finally this bizarre experiment leads him to discover the seven senses on which it suits him to meditate: *The person dissolves in the water of mirrors.*

Stephen is becoming lost because of his will to prove himself. Will he also discover that one understands only what one leaves behind? that one must emerge from himself to see himself as a whole? that courage is needed, and not mere complacency, not an impatient and yet vague desire for gratuitous comfort?

Modern man has a need to verify which loses its legitimacy as soon as it is expressed as the denial of what remains unconfirmable.

Stephen has no trust. The person is an act of faith; Stephen no longer knows what he is.

Apparently, he no longer knows how to love. (These young people do not want to tire themselves needlessly.)

This ridiculous story, nevertheless true, has been limited to the psychological side of a more profound adventure. It is good that the reader who fears having missed the true meaning of a text sometimes finds significant marks of his incomprehension. If the intimate rapport which connects the next sentence to the preceding considerations escapes you, my reader, you may find one of these signs. Stephen has forgotten the meaning of prayer.

Orpheus lost Eurydice because of mild skepticism, because of a scientific mind, because of methodical doubt—a mania to define, defiance of the gods, greed of the heart.

Each time we look in a mirror, we lose a Eurydice.

Mirrors might be death itself, absolute death which is not a new life, death in the frozen transparency of clarity, the clarity of the divided self.

One day, Stephen thinks feverishly: "All the mirrors should be broken. Then one could see himself *in truth*. Maybe one could recognize himself behind another face. Wouldn't forgetting one's face mean becoming a center of pure mind? or rather—and much better—a pure answer?"

It is a first, thin stream of fresh water piercing the arid soil, but Stephen does not yet hear the growl of deeper waters.

The desire to hypnotize himself still vaguely excites him. But he flees his own look, searching in other eyes, and that is why he frightens some women.

One evening, after a few drinks and an exchange of equally intoxicating thoughts with a friend whose beauty grows more and more striking, Stephen thinks he has caught in one of this woman's looks the echo of what he could be. All at once he loses himself in those eyes, as one dies in a birth.

Stephen is born into love and himself jointly. Many raptures have invaded him, silencing his reason and preventing him from protesting against this miracle.

Among all his mad words, names, kisses, calls which are their own answers, he repeats over and over, "I do not know. I am! . . . I don't know any more . . . but you are here!"

A little later, the sun dazzled all the glass of the capital. The windows were glinting. The sun and "death" were in league to lower all looks.* A restored Stephen was writing, "Your face hides all mirrors from me" to a woman he loved.

The Lost Shadow

The Enigma

In 1813, a wild-eyed character accosts Chamisso's imagination, refuses to give his name, and declares that he has lost his shadow.

The second romanticism is in full swing. Many madmen have been seen in Tieck's and Fouqué's works. This one, however, displays a more seriously disturbing sort of anxiety. "The man without a shadow" had been prowling the obscure regions of folklore for a long time. If he has risked appearing before Chamisso, it may be because he wants at last to be recognized, to be explained. For Chamisso was born French; a quirk of fate made him a German poet. Others have always believed in this fable but, as it were, without knowing it. Such is the reasoning of the man without a shadow. To surprise this Frenchman is to find his place in the sun, to confess his terrible secret! Often, a foreigner becoming acquainted with a people's beliefs is the first to be seized by the shiver of absurdity that is christened inspiration when it stirs or creates, within the person who experiences it, the desire to deliver himself of it by expressing it.

And this is how Chamisso came to introduce the myth of the man who has lost his shadow into the modern consciousness with the pathetic, naive features of the celebrated Peter Schlemihl. From Chamisso to Hofmannsthal, several writers have taken up this story. Hofmannsthal even mixed in some rather opaque science without damaging or fragmenting the mystery.

However, seeing so many authors exercising their imaginations on this subject makes one wonder why none of them has thought to justify himself. It is surprising that none of them ever tried to formulate the symbol contained in the myth. Could this be artistic modesty? or simple modesty? Or must one believe that they wrote their tales without ever asking themselves the meaning of an accident whose consequences are so picturesque that a "poet" (in the common sense of the word) would rather not know what caused it?

Finally, one wonders about the bond between the Teutonic

sphere and the literary expression of the myth: Chamisso, Andersen, Hofmannsthal, and many other imitators, among whom Hoffman is not the least important.

This enigma started to bother me during a stay in Germany during which I frequently observed the popularity of this good fellow Schlemihl. I was at the opera, and they were doing Strauss. I did not know Hofmannsthal's libretto and barely understood the plot of *The Woman Without a Shadow*. I saw an actress run across the stage shrieking. She was dragging behind her a large piece of cloth which represented her shadow and got in her way. During intermissions, people were talking about Freud. The music was vague, and it bored me. (Later I read the book, which I found splendid.)

"What is a shadow?" I asked myself. Something rather despicable. Latins ridicule it. For them it is unreality itself. ("He is a mere shadow of himself. . . . It is nothing, it is a shadow.") But they exaggerate. If we were pure mind, we would cast no shadow. The shadow is the humiliating proof of humiliating flesh —at least for those who, making a god of reason, would like to be taken for reasonable people. That is why, I thought, they despise the shadow and seriously underestimate it. But what else? They all have them, and they partake of the pleasures that the body bestows. They esteem transparency highly, but tolerate this flesh perfectly well—even those who deplore its becoming "opaque" under the gaze of lust. What could I draw from all this? Nothing but an obvious conclusion: The shadow is the reality of our flesh. But to lose one's flesh is to die, with all deference to the spiritualists, and this "unfortunate Schlemihl" did not die from losing his shadow. In fact, he was so much alive and his presence so disturbing that I attempted, in spite of the author, to force him into an ultimate confession. Psychoanalysis was available. Before resorting to such an extreme, I could have tried a less barbaric sort of pedantry. But by working hard to cast aside my heart's counsels of pity, I composed the following note.

The Psychology of Peter Schlemihl

Peter is a naive person; he believes in wealth. He believes above all that it alone assures man of dignity. He is a bourgeois of the most dangerous sort: the poor bourgeois who envies the rich bourgeois. Where does this feeling of inferiority come from? The Devil knows; that is how he gets his hold on him. Peter gives him his shadow for a magic purse with an inexhaustible supply of gold. Henceforth rich, but deprived of his shadow, he believes himself master of the world. But he is nothing of the sort. People make fun of him. Gratified, he is even more unacceptable than before. The inferiority complex that was scarcely routed by sudden fortune returns, and this time it is incurable. Before long it becomes a persecution complex. Everything frightens Peter and attacks him in a thousand ways. Children's street games, his valets, the women he meets, and especially daylight and moonlight. He searches for a solitary place to take his desperate thoughts. He often bursts into tears at the thought of the simplest happiness, the happiness whose secret everyone seems to be jealously and wickedly withholding from him. I say "secret" because it *is* a secret, like all the too natural things one has. Peter himself knows it, but only because he has sold it. (Doesn't one know what one has just lost? and lose what one knows, like Adam and Eve and innocence?)

Schlemihl is thus the classic type of the man who loses social contact. Even gold is not enough to reestablish such contact. Or rather, it apparently establishes it, but without reciprocity. The slightest test reveals this gap: People like Schlemihl for what he has, which is not himself. The women, of course, are the ones who guess it. What is the most real social relation? Let us assume that it is marriage, especially for this philistine. All of Peter's tricks fail when confronted with this last obstacle. In vain he goes to see his beautiful Mina only at night. When the day to sign the contract comes, when his deceit is brought out into broad daylight, Mina cries: "Oh! I was right! Yes, I have known it for a long time. He has no shadow!"

What is left for such a man? Suicide? Nothing is further from his mind. His vision of the world is exactly that of a likable philistine, of a philistine without demands, a philistine who would like to believe in virtue, if it were not for the void at his center. Like everyone else, except for that undefined something that is both nothing and everything, our misunderstood philistine finds himself driven from the society of his peers. It is his own fault! And there lies his bitterness. At this point flight intervenes. Out of a sense of thrift, he buys a pair of used boots. But here he is blessed with luck, for they are seven-league boots! From then on he escapes from life, intimacies, and conversation. His real existence blends with all the wanderings he imagines. He can even regain a sort of purely descriptive activity, solitary, almost mechanical. He complies a vast catalogue of all the plants in the world. And this is how he is occupying himself in Thebes, when the author and reader lose sight of him.

Inferiority complex, persecution complex, loss of social contact, guilt, a need to escape, manic activity (or the activity of an academic).

There is no doubt: Schlemihl is "schizoid." Chamisso, happily for him, knows nothing of this. Perhaps he knows something else.

An Attempt at Interpretation

For my part, I blame psychoanalysis for flattering our inclination to localize symbols. In spiritual life, there are no separate places. One can always move from one place to another by some trick of metamorphosis, which is how life is lived. Why say, then, that this caused that, when the reverse is at least as probable, and when things depend unquestionably only on everything? All this said, psychoanalysis can provide useful descriptions. I will, therefore, retain Freud's observation: "He who in any realm is considered abnormal from a social or moral point of view can be considered abnormal in his sex life."*

We have just seen that Schlemihl is the perfect "maladjusted" subject—one who cannot "find his place in the sun" and can only survive in the society of his peers by means of a subterfuge that is always threatened. From so total a social incompatibility we can deduce, it seems, a maximal aberration. To confirm our suspicions about the nature of this aberration, we should recall the following: Peter succeeds in hiding it from everybody except the two women he would like to marry. But let us not draw hasty conclusions.

Do the states of mind of a sick person or a madman differ essentially from those of a healthy person? Aren't they rather *fixations* of states which, normally, would quickly evolve into their opposites? More precisely, isn't Peter Schlemihl's state comparable to that of a healthy mind or body after lovemaking? For a few moments a man feels a sensation of emptiness, lightness, and at the same time heaviness, as if he lagged a little behind, slow to unravel the world to which he is returning and which burdens him with strange presences, sometimes sweet, but sometimes hostile. (And this state may be the first symptom of what will be called a persecution complex in a sick person.) This man also feels too lucid, piercing through everything and himself; hence the impression of being badly shielded from the looks he encounters—transparent, one would say, *without a shadow!* Here, possibly, is the first clue. It will, no doubt, be more convincing to adolescents than to adults, to melancholy people than to optimists. It would even be more convincing to Scandinavians than to southerners, we might add, with all the necessary reservations,* but keeping in mind the question we asked about the Germanic origins of the myth.

From the beginning, I had sensed that a fable so well known to a people must express a basic human fact. I was disappointed to see it reduced to something so precise, which a thousand prejudices, especially French, unite in ridiculing. A fragment written by Paracelsus that I happened to read at the time fortunately gave me the key to an infinitely richer and more disturbing interpretation. I will translate it literally: "One cannot compare the *Liquor Vitae* in man to anything except a shadow on a wall, which (shadow) comes from man and takes its shape from him. Such also is the *Liquor*, which is a microcosm; it is man's internal shadow."

A more advanced study by Paracelsus would soon teach me, along with many other strange and profound things, that the scope of this passage was actually much broader than all that could be imagined by this century's obtuse physiologism.

According to Paracelsus, the *Liquor Vitae* is in effect the principle of vital activity dispersed throughout our organs. It represents "the mirror in which nature contemplates itself within us." It is thus the microcosmic agent, the very power of creativity in all orders. It is "what is most noble in the whole body and in man." I would compare it to the German *Selbst*, or to the *Self* which Chamisso mentions at the end of his tale. This is what can finally pinpoint the real problem.*

Creativity! This is where everything serious in our life leads; and the notorious sexual question draws its exaggerated importance from the single fact that it is a physical image of general creative power.

As one can see by examining *modesty*, wouldn't this also be the reason that in many men creativity seems to reside in the sexual organs exclusively, and that modesty is localized there? Wouldn't this also be the reason that man tries to hide them like something sacred, and that Noah's sons covered the nakedness of their drunken father by walking backward toward him? But for the man who has become conscious of his spiritual mission, the center of creativity seems to move into the brain or heart. Modesty soon affects thought and feeling. One speaks of "exhibitionism" when an author is excessively sincere in his writings (even though he may be, in the usual sense of the word, the most prudish of all bourgeois: an H. F. Amiel). However, these remarks do not explain everything. To know one's deepest, most sacred secret, one's power to create, is normal; but it is apparently not normal to be ashamed of it. In fact, false modesty comes from the distinction between body and mind, from their ceasing to reflect each other. Then the body is ashamed of its thoughts, and the mind is ashamed of its body's desires, like an embrace without love or love without an embrace. And why does modesty cease, normally, when two people love each other? Because then the sexual organs regain their symbolic "propriety." (All that is shameful, dubious, and unclean is what is foreign to me.)

Let us return to our myth: Transparency is the absence of shadow, hence of secrecy. Now, if the "sacred" secret is the link to man's creativity, any man who has lost his shadow will walk among men in the anguish of seeing revealed in full daylight, not his secret, but his lack of a secret: his transparency. Spiritually or otherwise, he is no longer a creative man.

In the opposite sense, chastity (in body and in mind) renews man's enthusiasm for the world. It carries him ahead of everything, a little bit ahead of himself, where he can dominate his life and shape it, using all his instincts according to the image of his mind's vision. Body and soul sing in unison. The mind, aggressive and joyous, and the body, at ease in its skin, share the wealth of desire. And man has recovered his shadow.

Continuation and End of the Fable

Peter Schlemihl now seems a moving and accurate portrait of a romantic individual as a renouncer, one who cannot seize the world to form it to his image and who evades his vocation: the mystery of incarnation. Chamisso has given Peter all the physical and moral qualities of what will later be called the spleen of the soul, which is also the *spleen of the body*.

Hofmannsthal's novel—a poor imitation—describes the torment of a sterile woman, an empress who has lost her shadow and who borrows one from a common woman. Andersen, as one might expect, makes the "spiritual" aspect of the myth dominant. In his tale, *The Shadow*, the symbol of creative power has just detached itself from the author to take shape in his poetry. And afterwards, the poem, more beautiful and more alive than the man who conceived it, will return to submit to the poet.

It is one of the glories of German romanticism that it was able to raise man's weaknesses and some of his maddest illusions to the heights of myth or fable which are truer than life (richer in concrete lessons and invitations to metamorphosis). To give shape to what undoes us is the paradox of genius, the reluctant re-creative audacity of a Chamisso. Literary historians should avoid dulling such a work by admiring only a "gratuitous" whim of the imagination. There is no doubt that Chamisso's art is meaningful and is really great art, since any effort worthy of that name is first of all an ordering which gives life meaning. In this way Chamisso has been saved from himself. If he created Schlemihl, as we know, largely in his own image, he is nonetheless different from him, if only because he created him, evidencing a creative power whose novelty remains total. But I keep thinking—this eternal Schlemihl, this symbol in his seven-league boots who still crosses our lives, isn't he Chamisso's shadow? A shadow which, this time, has lost its man?

It is our century that has no more shadow. It no longer even knows how to write its own fable. It does not want to any more. It wants probability. It has sunk to the insignificant novel.*

Angérone

In disputing the mystery of love, some people forget themselves and define love in one or more ways. Why can't we love *love* enough never to have recourse to these remedies? For to define love is not to know it, but to limit its role in our lives, and no love can survive such suspicion or anxious greed.

But there is a conceivable way to speak of love without malice, by composing a few rhythms of phrases in which the unutterable emits a sort of emotion or uneasiness. Not that love is spoken or even described by allusions or symbols, but its sovereign presence is heralded by a quivering of the assembly of words which form its court: The king approaches.

All eloquence is amorous, stirred by a love which makes it blossom. But love itself is a thing of silence. What I cannot mention without offending it in its greatness is what inflames me to speak. Nothing can be said of love itself, but neither is anything said except of love, if anything is ever truly said.

In its own way, fable teaches us that love is the site of sacred silence. Angérone was the goddess of silence. It is believed that her statue was in the Temple of Voluptuousness, and some even think that she and the goddess Volupia are identical.

Let's take a look at this colloquy.

Voluptuousness is not pleasure itself, but the active imagination of desire slowly approaching its fulfillment. When desire seizes a man, it renders him speechless. This very muteness can even be the first manifestation of desire. One recovers speech only when desire is fulfilled and the mind is freed. Voluptuousness is a phenomenon analogous to hypnosis—a state in which the soul or mind focuses the range of man's faculties on a unique object in a single thought—identification through conquest by one person and surrender by the other.

That this hypnosis is to some extent—the mind's extent—independent of instinct is what the following two observations lead us to suppose. Extreme concentration of attention on a non-corporeal object, a work of art or a difficult thought, can be short-circuited by pleasure, while a vulgar or dissolute character bemoans the loss of voluptuousness.

A desirous man can only love *indefinitely*. He loves to stare for a long time in silence, to lose himself in someone's eyes (for hours, nights, dawns, moments). The budding intoxication of lovers is the silence that settles between them.

The meeting of lovers' eyes as soon as each accepts the undivided gaze of the other is comparable to vertigo. Judgment may remain free, but the soul turns outward and falls ceaselessly into this unique gaze. For a second or two it goes beyond time and hovers over a bottomless immobility. Then only a single eye can be seen in a face lost in shadows and slowly moving gleams, a single eye through which the entire soul peers and pleads with demanding tenderness. At still closer range, the eye loses all expression, an absolute gaze of anguish. If either of the lovers draws away at that moment, they are left wavering as if out of their senses. The lover takes his beloved's face in his hands and contemplates her. He repeats her name to himself, as if afraid. . . . Adolescence!

The spell of desire is the spell of silence; it endlessly postpones its fulfillment.

You hear only what stops. You know only what you lose. For what you want is not knowledge, but the divine awareness of the present. And this awareness is forbidden. It is lovers' closeness to violating the forbidden that imposes silence upon them, the fascination of sacred horror, the attraction of mortal fear.

In the silence of desire, possession has created a sudden roar of defiant, hostile waves. Now the smooth, low wave of a new moment surrounds us. For those who do not like the woman they have just possessed, silence dies at that very minute. They flee; they chat.

Platonic Sadness

In the fulfillment of the most violent love we are allowed to conceive of an absolute, but an inaccessible absolute. As soon as the limits of the power of desire are finally reached, in a couple's distracted solitude, Eros crowns them with icy despair: "You will not go beyond your unity."

Oh, silence of the stars! Are our souls melting? Two bodies fall asleep in their peace. Fulfilled at last, the lover does not know what to do with himself. He returns to himself and divides into his shadows. So pass the hours before dawn, in the uprooting of the soul and unutterable metamorphoses. Sometimes he wakes up completely, and his eyes imagine things in the dark: An embrace which would equal the infinite. A fusion into a single being, but a being that has access to its peers, that loves them, possesses them. Thus, through a succession of dizzy spells, multiplying amorous splendor, through a thousand successive embraces, he awakes to the desperately conscious, imaginary enjoyment of Being.

Dawn. The mind turns toward things and names them at a glance. A body close to mine is breathing, a heavy memory of an incommensurable night. We shall not go beyond ourselves. But in this defeat of our embrace, isn't there a memory of the only wilderness we will ever seek?

At the end of our escape, we shall never reach anything but a fascinating impossibility. And we shall live from that moment in the dizziness of destroying ourselves as we touch this infinite, which is more powerful than joy and sadness, in the dizziness of returning to touch this absolute, which can be sensed only by the person who experiences it to the edge of terror—the being that we form at the height of love and that dies at the instant it is born.

Our Platonism collapses at the end of the embrace. Then the symptoms of love (shall we say) change. We suddenly realize that desire was the dialogue of bodies, while pleasure is solitary, the moment when lovers are the most separate, torn, and withdrawn. Pleasure is the end of the dialogue, not the dreamed-of fusion. It brings with it the consciousness, seriousness, and reality of our lives. We are two.

There are only two philosophies: that of the desire and that of the act. Or rather, there are only two doctrines: that of silence and that of speech.

The negation of amorous desire by the act that fulfills it is the physical, primitive sign of the infinite contradiction that afflicts us. Desire makes us divine; the act makes us human. Dreamed-of love dies at the threshold of the love which is our true task.

Let us leave this temple where two idols sleep and speak the language of day.

A Contribution to the Study of Love at First Sight

One look meets another, and suddenly they are riveted, rooted to the spot, as a rooster is glued to the chalk line drawn in front of his beak. It would be too stupid if it were not too beautiful. But it is useless not to believe in it. It is a fact. We have all been through it, and we all have said, "I can't help it." And we have said it as sincerely, it seems to us, as a believer describing his conversion to grace and predestination. Yet, if it is useless to deny the fact, it is not useless to question its fatalistic nature. Isn't the helplessness we allege really an excuse?

Here I am speaking only of real love at first sight, the kind that starts a fire. For the loves that we wait for or invite are nothing but heat lightning in a stormy heart. At the door of a passing train, between two stations, or in a crowd where eyes are trying to meet—they turn away as soon as they touch, and it is always, "Oh, I would have loved you!" But no. If it were true, I would have been able to stop you. And the whole world would have changed at that moment, without anyone's suspecting.

I was skeptical in those days. I was telling a certain novelist (one of the best in Germany): "The myth of love at first sight is undoubtedly one of Don Juan's wily inventions to make an impression on his victims. He talked about it so much, and so have all of you after him, that every woman who encounters it is on the lookout for the slightest signal that this apparition might arouse in her. How easy to persuade a woman, once she is so interested! For nothing is more flattering than the idea that you are going to relive a scene from a novel. Yes, the idea alone has caused all this devastation, not some god or fate. There would never be love at first sight were it not for the desire that you keep alive through your novels.

"But an acquired willingness is not enough. One also needs an encounter contrived like a dream: a complete ritual, with assigned roles, an overture trumpeted by a herald, an impressive ceremony which prevents you from running away. Just think of the unrelenting pomp surrounding the classic encounters: Tristan at the Court of Ireland is received by the king's daughter according to custom and etiquette. Siegfried and Brunhilde walk toward each other in the hanap scene like officiating priests. Everything happens as if the lovers were chosen, not by blind fate, but on the contrary by the consummate fitness of their social roles, under the aegis of an intangible hierarchy. And Don Juan is cheating again when he pretends that it happens unexpectedly, by surprise. An image comes to mind whose clarity excuses its prosaicness: Love at first sight, in spite of its name, is not a snapshot, but a portrait."

As I talked, something started to bother me. I felt that I was speaking out of turn. My remarks seemed to touch my companion too personally, and—how should I say it—he seemed to know better than I the story I was telling him.

"Allow me," he said kindly, "to answer you with a confession. I don't know, though, what one can conclude from it for or against your theories.

"At the beginning of 1933, when Hitler was coming to power, I was invited to give some lectures in Budapest. The president of the organization that invited me was an important banker and a friend of the arts. He met me at the airport and drove me to his home. It was lunch time. We had been chatting for some time in his library (where in a furtive glance I had noticed my books) when his wife came in, greeting us with a melodious Hungarian phrase. Once we were introduced, she suggested the ritual of peach brandy, in which you drink three glasses at one gulp while looking each other in the eye. I felt myself pale violently.

"We proceeded to the table. Soon my host became concerned: 'You look pale and you haven't eaten a thing! Do you feel ill?' I stammered something about my flight. The banker understood that quite well. He talked a lot to comfort me, told me excitedly how he had organized my lectures, what audience I would have, and who was asking me to dinner. In short, you remember what Hungary was like, that incomparable hospitality, that lyrical freedom in relations. . . . But it did no good. I couldn't swallow a single bite. Was it really due to the flight? I was ready to believe it when I noticed, and not without terror, that the banker's wife had not touched her food either.

"Anyway, the lunch ended without my host's noticing that my disease was contagious. He went on talking while we had coffee and then apologized for having to go back to the bank. Besides, his wife would show me around Buda and take me to the museum—see you tonight! He left, very pleased with himself and with me as well, I think. We were alone.

"Silence. Silence again in the car, which she drove with an expression of intense, almost angry concentration. We drove through the broad avenues of Pest, the Chains Bridge over the yellow waters of the Danube, then through those narrow streets of Buda which climb the sides of an enormous rock right in the middle of the city, dominated by a statue of Saint Gellert with his arms extended. She stopped the car at the gate of a public park, got out, and walked off in the frozen snow, which her steps slowly penetrated and tracked. I joined her. She pointed out the city at our feet: 'My husband asked me to show you Budapest. Here is Budapest.'

"There was nothing else to say. We got back into the car and drove down toward the city. All of a sudden, I made up my mind and said, 'You ate nothing at lunch, Madam.' 'Neither did you.' I continued, not without difficulty, 'How about having something in a restaurant?' 'Good idea,' she answered in a low voice, without looking at me.

"Soon we were seated before red caviar sandwiches. And it started all over again. The same thing as at lunch. Neither of us could eat a thing.

"Suddenly I stood up. I walked around the table and stopped

in front of her, with my arms behind my back, this way—I stopped myself from touching her shoulder—and I heard myself saying, 'Since this has to happen, well . . . let it happen!'

"She got up and followed me. We went to her house. Dizziness, somber delirium, and without a word being spoken. . . . And it went on that way during my entire stay in Budapest. In the afternoons, I told you, we never talked. In the evenings, I had my lectures or a dinner party. And I spent the rest of the nights in a bar with an exiled painter named Maria. I had met him a few years earlier in Berlin in a political group which I had joined without my wife's knowledge.

"I was in a state of extreme exaltation, almost incapable of sleeping, except for a few hours in the mornings. With my friend Maria I discussed art, religion, politics, the prospects of the new regime, but nothing about my afternoons, of course.

"The day before I was to leave, as Maria and I were leaving the bar, a morning edition of the paper carried a headline about the Reichstag fire. I decided to return to Berlin that day and said good-by to my painter friend, who was very concerned about me. He had reason, for at that time I was a member of the Communist party. I learned that the plane would leave at ten in the morning. But I had to see *her* again for the last time. So I decided to take the evening train.

"I arrived in Berlin the next day. On the doorstep of our villa in Zehlendorf, my wife was waiting, grim and almost harsh. I wasn't thinking about anything but the political situation. We sat down at the table, and I asked her anxiously about the events of two days ago. She hardly answered. What is it?

" 'The one you cheated with. Who was she?' she finally asked.

"I looked at her a long time, straight in the eye. No doubt about it, she knew. I can keep a state secret, as you know, but I cannot tolerate a lie in my private life. I confessed everything without trying to make excuses. And since she remained silent, I asked her how she had found out. Then she handed me an airmail letter addressed to me, which had arrived the same morning. She had opened it, fearing disastrous news about me. All she found were a few lines on notepaper with the letterhead of a bar in Budapest: 'Send news quickly. I am worried about you. I will never forget those extraordinary nights we could still spend together, on the eve of this cataclysm.' The letter was signed 'Maria.' "

"A real drama of fate!" I said after a while. "The true *Schicksalsdrama*, as you call it. But doesn't the blind destiny that presided over your encounter lose some of its mystery when you know that the banker's wife read novels—and most probably your own novels? And did not this love at first sight come from a heaven that should be called Literature?"

Fame

We knew him slightly and thought we knew him well. His posthumous papers show that he was quite different. It was to be expected, of course; yet we cannot get over our surprise. It's just that everything in his books—especially the most sincere of them—seemed to exclude the preoccupations his diary reveals. Perhaps the secret of this strange difference is hidden in the passages from those notebooks transcribed here. We cannot draw any clear conclusions from these variously dated fragments; there are too many contradictions. But that's what may be interesting. Such a deeply equivocal attitude toward fame must maintain the strangest misunderstandings between an author and his readers. This may even be the attitude of most modern writers.

"I used to live for glory," says Prince Andrey. "And what is glory? The same love for others, the desire to do something for them, the desire for their praise. In that way, I lived for others, and not almost, but quite spoiled my life. And I have become more peaceful since I live only for myself. Others, one's neighbors, as you and Marie call them, they are the great source of error and evil. One's neighbors are those—your Kiev peasants—whom one wants to do good to" (Tolstoy, *War and Peace*).

This passage had charmed me with its ill temper. As I copy it now I find nothing in it but sophistry. No, glory is not love of your neighbor, but scorn. Prince Andrey found no neighbors, because he sought only an audience. An audience gives glory to those who scorn it enough to flatter it. Princess Marie, who really did love her neighbor, received no glory from the public and asked none. And she didn't think she had "spoiled her life."

At the end of a triumphant concert, Liszt bows and says quietly, "I am the servant of the public, that goes without saying." That is the sort of thing to which glory is granted. And those who do not court it run a serious risk of being disliked. The masses have never thought it ridiculous for someone to display a love of fame, even if it is exessive compared with his talents.

The masses consider glorious only those who bother to speak of their glory. Chateaubriand was glorious, but not Stendhal. Mme. de Staël was, but not Benjamin Constant (as a writer). Yet no one reads Chateaubriand's *Martyrs* or Staël's *Corinne* any more, and everyone thinks he likes the *Charterhouse* and *Adolphe*. But this altered opinion of their talent has brought about no change in opinions about their fame. Thus, fame is a myth. By that I mean that its power and grandeur do not come from any sort of reason, or even allow it. "Reputation grows with time, presence only diminishes it." All fame is mad. Chateaubriand's fame belongs neither to him nor to his work, but to his audience, who loan it to him because the author lent himself to them first. As for me, I am too proud to play that game. I would feel dispossessed. I want to be loved for myself, just as I am, and not as their sentimental taste for "Art" would have me.

But how complicated and contradictory things are! Can it be that he who wants fame lacks pride? Could he be more humble than I? And isn't my pride proof of love for my public in demanding more nobility of it? To say, "I do not care for glory" is to say, "I do not care for you, who give glory in return for flattery." But it is also a way of saying, "I love you, for I wish you were less vulgar than you are." Doesn't he who refuses the glory a crowd gives its flatterers wish for a glory he alone could bestow?

The modern idea of glory comes, they say, from the Renaissance. Glorious is he who asserts himself by being different, rather than by excelling. Thus it is the *individual* who distinguishes himself, in whatever domain. (Crimes committed for the sake of glory were frequent in fifteenth-century Italy.) The need for glory is thus born of a sort of malady of social consciousness. It is the opposite of brotherly love. The individual who seeks glory neither cares about nor notices the neighbor he might help, but only the neighbor he might use. He seeks admirers, *con-*

firmers of his being. Setting oneself apart from a communion or a community sets one apart from oneself as well, so one feels the need of confirmation.

A man actively communing with those around him would not think of seeking glory, since glory creates separation. He would rather seek excellence in his place, according to his stars. Thus heroes and kings are authors of their own renown. They give, and ask for nothing. And their gifts create their people's reputation. (Today we see the opposite: The crowd's gifts create a man's glory.)

Ancient glory was gratuitously virile. Exemplary Alexander, fairest of all, strongest and happiest of all, was not set apart, but stood at the summit. His glory was in his destiny, measured by a universal standard that his actions met precisely. But our glory knows no standard; it is a rumor, publicity, a sort of temporary magnification. It is not grand, but exaggerated, changeable, excitable, sentimental. And what's worse, it is felt as flattery. Thus, it is vulgar. In fact, I know of no modern glory whose source cannot be demonstrated to be a vulgar deed. (Zones of baseness in d'Annunzio: It is that, and not the beauty of his work, which constituted his glory.)

And yet I have caught myself wishing for a glory which would not weigh upon me—not theirs, but one I could reach, glory as I and I alone have always known it to be.

A god needs no worshipers to shine and rejoice in his being. Yes, that is indeed a god's privilege. And true glory.

What does "incognito" mean? Someone is worth something; no one knows it. Glory today is pretty much the opposite. But might that not also be the best way of remaining incognito, precisely by appearing to seek fame?

Another advantage to fame: It gives one the right to be banal. So what if that right is often abused?

A hypothesis: Intimate experience of fame always precedes its manifestation.

An ambitious man is not destined for fame. He can attain only success. He remains the slave of comparison.

Many men do not think it possible to admit to vanity, or they believe it would be naive. And yet if one admits one's arrogance, they take that to be vanity.

I am a man, and therefore vain, naive, cunning, arrogant, et cetera. What's the use of hiding these traits? The most stupid of vanities is certainly to try to make people believe that you are not vain. If you want to disavow your own vanity, the best way to be rid of it would be to speak of it openly—the way a liar might say, "I warn you that I am about to tell a lie, for such-and-such an easily verifiable reason." It would be instructive and amusing.

I desire my fame, and I never admit it. I act modestly. Why such a sense of propriety?

I do not want glory to dazzle you with, you whom I love, you who know me. You know what I am, and if someday you were to learn that I am famous, what essential thing would you know that you do not know now? Or else you would be making a mistake, believing others where you do not believe yourself—and I do not want error. Or do I want *that* error?

I do indeed want it, but not as an error.

What then is "glory," whose name, with as little importance as I grant it, brings tears to my eyes? Glory and light, glory and mystery, glory and luminous death, glory and that triumphant chord, or rather the moment on the threshold of its resolution—what is that threshold, and what do symphonies reveal; onto what heaven do they open?

I dare not say I would be God. But that would be *my* truth, the truth of my falsehood. Is it because my name is *falsehood* that I want fame and do not know why? Or do not dare know why?

What I dare not know is anguish. Anguish is the name of the secret I serve without daring to serve it, because I know that its name is falsehood, and that it is I who am nothing.

Thus, God is my adversary. He alone opposes my glory and saves me from my triumph in spite of myself. There is only one God, the one who says I Am. It shall be God or it shall be myself. If it is myself, it shall be nothing. If it is God, I shall be nothing. If God kills me, he will be everything, and everything will be. Thus, oh Lord, deliver me from fame!

But that prayer moves me just as fame does.

Retying the Gordian Knot

An oracle had foretold that someone would gallop at full speed, standing in his chariot, into Jupiter's temple, and he would be king. The few who knew of this prediction were excluded from competition by their very knowledge; spiritual innocence was required. As for the people, they tended to their work.

One day, a peasant by the name of Gordius came to that Phrygian town. He announced that he wanted to visit the local points of interest. The temple and the town hall were pointed out to him. Without hesitating, he entered the temple standing in his chariot, and the priests cried out in unison: "He is king! Behold the long-awaited king!"

Having become king by accident and the grace of innocence, Gordius wanted to remain king through the ingenuity of a craftsman. He leaped to the ground, determined to demonstrate his prowess to the townspeople. Between the horns of the altar and the shafts of his chariot, he fell to tying the most beautiful knot he had ever imagined. He spent indescribable hours of intensity and concentration on it. He had the time of his life! The knot is there to prove it. The innocence of the predestined man and the craftiness of the peasant are blended in a swirl of invention, a tangle of genius.

The most artful loops of the cord tie ambition to grace, wed ingenious greed to mad luxury, and bind the excitement and anguish of greatness in the chains of instinctive calculation. By Jupiter, the fellow who's clever enough to untie this crude masterpiece hasn't been born yet!

We know nothing of Gordius' reign. But the knot he tied became famous. A new oracle soon sanctified it among the Greeks: Whoever could untie it would rule over all of Asia.

A knot is first of all a ring, a symbol of betrothal and seizure of power—magic circle and royal crown. It is also a sign of fertility. Once a plot is knotted, it rules all the characters who live it. Marriage and friendship have their ties. When we say that a fruit has knotted, we mean it has gone to seed.

The man who knows how a knot is tied also knows how to untie it and retie it. He holds the secret of power.

From every region of Greece, those who dream of crowns came to contemplate the knot. They came and sat before it to study it passionately for hours, days, months. How many great thoughts were tied to that trap for symbolic meditation! And how many apparently idiotic stares learned to decipher the convolutions of that symbol of the brain, born of a unique and truly sovereign thought: royalty in its nascent state.

I remember. I used to go to the temple on days when I was uncontrollably angry. I shot glances like arrows at that phlegmatic vipers' nest. Profound vengeance lay coiled in the scarcely visible twistings that I imagined inside the monstrous thing, *made of a single cord.*

And I spent hours contemplating those who, like myself, contemplated the Gordian Knot.

One man carried the knot within himself and was in analysis at Delphi. Between sessions, he came secretly and crouched down with us, his helpless fascination retying everything the priest had untied, retying the knot as nature had tied it, loving it because it was his nature.

Another forecast modern science. He told me, "There is no science outside those phenomena that can be reproduced at will. What is this knot—real, unique, inimitable—this unquestionable object that science will be unable to test or unravel for lack of the formula to duplicate it? In the eyes of science, it does not exist. Science will have nothing to do with it. And if nobody will have it, it is mine! I take it. It is my liberty."

One man murmured from time to time, "It is consoling!" He was referring to his misfortunes in love, which were so simple.

One day Gordius' wife came to discharge her religious duties.

In front of the knot, after a long stare, she said, "It's not *that* good a likeness!" She thought she was her husband's only concern.

And many others came and stayed a long time. And none left without becoming one mystery richer. That was the cult of Gordius, a religion of the inextricable.

Alexander, crafty and impatient, entered the temple on the day his stars dictated, sliced through the knot with a stroke of his sword, and garnered the trophy for the rest of the season. (All players lose.)

That sword stroke founded the modern world, a world of hasty simplification, experiments which destroy their subject, efficient action at the expense of judgment, cheating, broken ties.

And since then I have gone forth crying, "Retie it! Retie it! For everything is at stake, the very meaning of life!"

For you are dying, we are all dying of boredom, in a world where nothing knots.

For you are dying, we are all dead in spirit, in what is valuable. Life is formed only in the complexity of a soul, in the twistings of the deepest secret ever tied. And if you simplify, you will win the world, but at the price of a soul, your own.

For you are dying, we all are nearly dead to love, which severs nothing, but espouses, accepts, penetrates, and knows that to tie a solid bond, you need all those illogical twists and turns, all that hopeless intricacy, those infinite folds which defy calculation.

For a cross section of a knot teaches us almost nothing of its structure, but forever destroys the hope of re-creating it, understanding it, or giving oneself to it, knowing or loving.

The only story which we may contrast with the myth of the Gordian Knot is the story of the Simplest Knot in the World.

In the fifteenth century, civil war was about to break out

among the Swiss. A messenger was sent to the Hermit of the Alps, who ruled over the Swiss though he had no power. At that last moment, having lost all hope, the people asked his advice. He took the rope which was the belt of his shabby robe. He made a simple loop in it and gave it to the messenger. "Give them this knot," he said, "and tell them to untie it."

"A feeble child could untie that!" exclaimed the messenger.

"The strongest men could not untie it," answered the Hermit. "It will have to be cut with a sword, as long as each man keeps pulling one end of the rope toward himself."

"What an edifying story," said Alexander.

The Torment of Tantalus

Water flees his lips, the branch flees his hand, and the boulder hanging over his head is about to fall, but never does. To an unenlightened observer, it seems that Tantalus' desire is enough to repel the things he wants, and his apprehension enough to keep at bay the things he fears. When he leans toward the surface of the river which immerses him to the waist, when he reaches toward the ripe fruits that bend the branch above his head, it is as though his very gesture triggers a mechanism which cancels it out. But it also seems that when he turns his anguished glance toward the boulder, it keeps the boulder in place. A strange place, this little corner of hell, where the weighty logic of matter is abolished by a man's slightest motion. Can this be one of those places where mind rules? Yes, for at the very moment when Tantalus is aroused, when he makes a plan, when he acts, the laws of falling bodies and the laws of inertia, which are the laws of death, yield to the laws of the gods, which are the laws of the spirit, the laws of gods who are angry at man, the laws of a guilty spirit.

Let us take a good look at this imaginary landscape, this composition, simplified like a tarot card, and no less charged with symbols: a body, water, a branch, and a rock. It is man in his guilt, surrounded by the emblems of his fear and lust, emblems or symbols, for everything here depends on interior events. Everything depends on man, and everything illustrates one of the basic forms of his being.

According to the fable, Tantalus had committed two crimes. Having been admitted to the gods' table, he had stolen his hosts' nectar and ambrosia so that mortals might taste them. Then, to defy Olympus and test his omniscience, he had killed his own son Pelops to serve his flesh at the divine table.

Here the liquors of immortality are like signs of grace, which a man might try to seize through subterfuge, to guarantee himself an empire on earth. We must doubt that philanthropy was the motive for Tantalus' theft, since he was clearly jealous of the gods, of their soothsaying, their power, and all the pleasures those things gave them.

As for the execution of his son, offered to the gods as a better food, it is startling to note that it is an exact inversion of the sacrifice of the Son of God. Instead of the Father delivering his Son to men that they might kill him, but also that they might live again by consuming his spiritual body, Tantalus killed his son himself and gave his flesh to the gods that they might die of it— if they lose their divinity by having once been surprised and fooled.

Corresponding to that double infraction of the graces of the spirit (as I like to call spiritual laws) is a punishment in which we can detect a dual reflection of the crime in a human medium. Because he envied the food of the gods, Tantalus is refused the food of men. His jealousy is reflected in the frustration of desire. And his challenge to heaven, having failed, is inverted in a suspended threat.

The pagan world conceives of neither grace for the sake of love nor gratuitous salvation, and that is why punishments inflicted by the gods generally take on the character of revenge— pure, simple, and apparently automatic. In other words, in the pagan world, man remains alone with himself and is insulated against the interventions of a transcendent force, or a summons from beyond. (The "gods" are, in fact, nothing but his own limits.)

In the story of Tantalus' torment, this automatic revenge is so obvious that it warrants precise—though apparently fantastic —speculation.

I see Tantalus upheld in the river, the boulder suspended over his head, the waters and the branch hovering nearby until the instant he tries to reach them. All of this really *depends* only on him, on the inclinations of his soul, which have not changed since he committed his crimes. Stubbornly cherishing the same desires and the same pride, he feeds the vengeance of the "gods" who frustrate those desires and who are ironically slow to crush that pride.

Let us now imagine the impossible: that Tantalus might give up for a moment, that he might let himself go, and that he might suddenly prefer, instead of his love of a guilty and tortured self, liberating expiation and its joy. At that very instant, the river engulfs him, he drinks his death, and the rock crushes him.

But this is precisely what never happens, and never can happen, in Tartarus.

Because he does not believe in resurrection or grace or the salvation that an instant of pure release would afford (he would pay with his life, of course, but what an indescribable rebirth!), Tantalus *prefers* to submit to the torture of Tantalus. It is his pride and his human dignity; he is in revolt against everything except himself.

That is why nothing around him changes.

Let us now consider the Man of Desire, Tantalus symbolically reduced, in the legend, to his hunger, his thirst, and his fear. He is the man in each of us who prefers desire, even if painful after thousands of disappointments—but still *his* desire, and thus himself—to the prize he can win only by agreeing first to be changed. "What would be the use," he thinks, "of winning the world, if it means losing my self?" There can be no doubt that in his way he is right. For winning always means losing something: anticipation, hope, longing. Imagine a person who has desired for so long that his whole being has become anticipation, hope, and longing. That being would die—necessarily, by definition—if the gift were given. Or else a new being would spring forth at the moment the gift was given to receive it in his place.

At the worst, and in the logic of a myth wherein man is identified with one of his longings, the one who wins is always *another*. And the one who desires will never win.

It is the emperor's fallacy: Napoleon is not Bonaparte fulfilled, but someone who has taken Bonaparte's place under the ermine cloak. The romantic who dreamed of being emperor died on coronation day.

All our successes, and probably all our *acts*, are therefore to some extent changes of identity, alienations of ourselves. At worst, they are also usurpations.

Let us now change spiritual planes and transport the myth of Tantalus into a world in which the instant of release no longer means death but life, and the legacy of eternal life. I will borrow a parable from Jean-Paul* which in a deeply humorous vein reproduces our Greek fable, but with a happy ending.

Uncle van der Kabel has died, and in the presence of his seven natural heirs, a lawyer opens and reads the will. The last article is drawn up thus:

"All my goods, whatever they be, shall accrue and belong to the one of my seven nephews who, in the half-hour following the reading of this article, shall be the first to shed one or several tears for me, his late uncle, in the presence of a respectable magistrate who will sign an affidavit to that effect. If all eyes remain dry, my worldly goods shall be given to the residuary legatee named below."

At that point, the lawyer puts his watch on the table (it shows half past eleven) and waits for the tears. Neupeter, the merchant, wonders whether this is a practical joke, unworthy of a sensible man. Knol, the tax collector, feels ready to shed tears of anger. Pasvogel, the crafty bookseller, tries to recall all the touching things that books have in them. Klitte, who is Alsatian, swears that for all the gold in the world, a joke of this sort would not make him cry, whereupon Harprecht, the police inspector, points out that if he managed to cry from laughing it would simply be a case of theft. But the Alsatian replies that if he laughs, "it is out of pure humor, with no more serious intent." The inspector opens his eyes wide, and no tears flow. The young preacher, Flachs, would be inclined toward ecclesiastical lamentation, but the vision of his uncle's house coming toward him over the waves is much too cheering. Glanz, the churchwarden, launches into a speech, because he knows that always makes him cry. But now Flachs has closed his eyes. He thinks of his Uncle van der Kabel, of his gifts, his gray frock coats, then of Lazarus and his dogs, of a lot of different faces, the sorrows of young Werther, a small battlefield, and at last himself. He tortures himself so pitifully over the will that he comes close to crying. The warden continues his speech. Suddenly Flachs rises to his feet and says, "I believe, honorable gentlemen, that I am crying!" And indeed, he sobs briefly as he sits down. His emotion having been duly recorded, he will inherit all his uncle's goods because he gave him a single thought—among so many others—springing from pure and gratuitous love.

The author of the New Testament asks no more of man for the inheritance of his kingdom. He asks a moment's faith, an instant of self-release, of disinterested love.

Any attempt to *deserve* the Kingdom and the Life, which are offered for nothing, automatically starts up the mechanism of Tantalus' torture: It cancels itself out.

If a man thinks he can justify himself by the merit of his works, he will not cry, for the vision of the approaching prize will be "much too cheering" for his heart, and the desired kingdom will at once become distant, like the branch burdened with fruit.

If a man wants eternal life simply out of fear of dying in this life, the Living Water will flee his lips. For to be immersed in that water, one must be willing to die for one's desires and oneself. (That is the symbol of Baptism.)

Such is the game of unfathomable Love. Let us admire its miraculous precision! For if the least egotism remains in the act of bringing one's lips or hand to that water, to that waiting fruit, then love of self still dominates pure Love, and the anticipated pleasure still suffices to hold back the tear which alone, and in a single instant, can earn eternal joy.

The End of the World

Among all the liberties thought takes when, detaching itself from our situation, it conceives ideas for destroying man, we face without too much fear the idea of man destroyed; the idea of man thinking the idea, destroyed; the idea that you who are thinking one day will no longer exist, that one day you will be a dead man.

If "macabre" is the word for the strangeness of others' deaths, it can never be applied to one's own death—to my own. Nor do I think it can be applied to the meditations I am pursuing between these sentences on this nondescript morning, typically ordinary, when fatigue could not make me consider stopping. But what if everything should come to an end for me before noon? I don't think this is a tragic idea; it belongs to me, I may do as I wish with it, pretend rather easily to laugh at it. It is no stronger than I. It may even be simply a transparent ruse of my vitality: The very idea that in a few moments my breath could stop makes me breathe faster.

And that does not mean that we have never thought of death with sudden terror—we think of it more often than we dare believe, we probably think of nothing else—but we have never been able to imagine our own death. To entertain the idea would be to admit openly that we cannot fully understand the word "to imagine." For to imagine one's own death realistically would be to die at once. Perhaps this is the only criterion of intellectual perfection, and we see why its application can be neither reported nor repeated. Perfection and death are the same in being absolutely tragic, that is, beyond appeal.

Ontology of the End

For us to see the strangeness of such a situation—which all of us share—a mysterious event must magnetize our thought and focus it upon what the natural world will not take seriously. For if we remain impotent to imagine our deaths as long as we live, this phenomenon should normally be considered negligible; to spend any more time on it would be gratuitous sophistry. My nature cries out against utopia when confronted with my death. That is why humanity as a whole instinctively resists the thought of the End, refuses with all its strength to make it real, even works to disqualify it, to render it abstract and distant, to chase it forever into an indefinite future. So it is with man, so with humanity. Yet one day, one ordinary day, the man dies.

Why am I stirring these things up? It is true that these are the only ideas which grow more interesting with time, if we grant that time always runs in the same direction—toward its end. But that is a poor reason. Since that is how it runs, measured out in regular seasons, time has made us numb rather than warn us of its end. If one day man learned the truth about his fate and his freedom, if he saw with the naked eye their final meaning and what was really at stake, who would rule the world, the Preacher or the Young Man? The wise man would ridicule with no less envy the profligate, whose second thoughts and inability to choose once and for all would still be pitiful. To live is impure, whether or not we know life's direction, and that is why good reasons explain not our reality, but only that which condemns it. Thus, there are the best reasons in the world to think of the End, though all the efforts of our life neutralize it.

What is the source of this sudden recognition of both the threat and man's inability to imagine his end concretely? Why is it that, imperceptibly for most of us (and for all mindless literati), the thought of catastrophe is slowly settling in? Why, if not because of the end already penetrating us, if not because of the reality that goaded me to write these pages and that could end my sentence here and hurl me to my judgment? If it occurs to us to imagine our deaths, it is Death in us thinking of itself, it is the Crisis welling up, warning us of the End and attesting to it.

The Crisis

At the time, the "decline" of the Roman Empire was a decline only to those who saw it in the light of a new reality. Without life, what can we say of death? And without the End, what can we say of continuity? But everything remains confused. We are here as in a dream, entangled in a feeling of urgency which we cannot distinguish no matter how wide we open our eyes. It is enough for anguish, but not enough for action. Thus the great declaration of crisis which is raging through the heart of this century is only a first word, and an ambiguous one, spoken by the End. A first petition. It is not the final decree, but the decline that makes us obscurely aware of an immediate danger, the twilight that may be a dawn, and the corona of the shock which will consume all flesh.

Some day the real face of the earth may appear in this suspect light. And already, intermittently, a few of us have caught a glimpse of the real goals of our age-old journey and have tried to judge them.

What do we know of the meaning of our civilization? What has been its goal, from the beginning, what is its dream? Greatness? We have destroyed all standards. Nothing is either great or small now, but everything defies us to surpass it. Liberty? We have cluttered the entire planet with barriers designed to guard its course. Love? Fellowship? Those are the ideals of leagues, words which we now dare use only over dessert. Wealth? It is no longer within the reach of human hands. It is only a number designating distant powers. And yet it remains linked to the dream of activity which has tortured the West for centuries. But, in its turn, this dream is growing cloudy; it is weakening; it no longer encompasses the breadth of human consciousness.

Our will is no longer to conquer, but only to insure the lives of the greater number against the catastrophic creations of the heroes and great neurotics. Recently fear has begun to rule us. We are trying (in the banal phrase of moralists that is beginning to take hold) to evaluate future conquests. This is a clear sign that we fear them. (What if time, from now on, were working against us?) The whole world is organizing itself at the average standard of living which seems to offer the fewest opportunities to death, or to any creative act. A vast insurance network stretches over our activities: plans and pacts, statistics on the unexpected, eugenics and longevity, intellectuals brought to heel or sterilized, war outlawed, security first and foremost. We are not learning to die any more, we are learning to live. This effort is contrary to nature. It is born as life declines and inevitably turns against life. We want to escape from time, from its threat; but it may be the best way, or the only way, to anticipate the end of time: the end of time, the End of the World. For it may well be that the global insurance we are trying to organize will bring about our collective ruin. Once the whole earth has submitted to the power of statistics alone and depends on a single control panel, the Angel of the End need only seize the controls, and time will be over.

And we will be taken by surprise, as no other generation would have been. For as time passes, the closer its end, the less our faith, the less vigilant our watch. The early church, at the beginning of our age, lived with the thought of an imminent end. We thought we could force that tragic dimension from our lives, but ironically fate has taken it upon itself to reinforce it. That fate is not time, but our own efforts. For the first time in the history of the world, we can calculate the cost of destroying humanity: the total of our national defense budgets.

Warning

Your refuge is in the masses and their history. You say secretly that the masses cannot die, and it is true that they have no real life and therefore cannot imagine their end or anything else. They themselves cannot be contemplated, and the man within them is nearly devoid of reality until the End contemplates him. That is his tragedy, and the End's comedy.

Everything real, everything that manifests the eternal presence of the End, everything that gives a sense of eternity to your antics, you call exaggerated, inflated. Listen to me. What if the world were really lost, no matter how much you wanted it to survive or how strongly you believed it would last as long as you? *What if the truth were totally inordinate?* Who would die in shame and rage?

Those who still believe in standards and seek their strength in illusion will fall by the thousands into the void. But those who have seen and have believed their eyes will, in the storm, reaccustom themselves to high slopes. For only he who accepts death is not vertigo's plaything.

The time is coming when men will no longer have to defend themselves, but only to reveal themselves as they are, wherever they may be.

No more spiritual evasion. Man, fleeing the earth where the devil rages, seeks refuge on the heights and discovers that God is more dangerous there, different, attended by lightning.

Vicissitude

The world's stage set has just shifted to a vast conversation about death, in the squares and in the cafés, in public places where people talk quickly. Perhaps the dead sun will soon move through the dirty sky. Who would go out and look? I alone am surprised: Can our world slide by so easily? Can everything be changed, and men go on with their speeches, forgetting their horror? These days, we must believe it possible. It happens like a dream, or sudden anger, or springtime, or nightfall. (A first lamp is lighted. Someone says, "It's here.")

67

First Judgment, by Light

The indisputable End of the World halted a little way ahead of its followers, looked at them severely, then began to move again, keeping the same scornful distance. But the majority managed to keep on looking as though they did not believe that their death was close. Surely they'd get over the end of the world! If not, everything would be unspeakably indecent. The year 1000 had passed nearly a thousand years ago—"and all its prayers wasted"—but they knew that nothing could end totally and forever, except at a cost which it was forbidden to imagine. People who have learned good manners don't like to see them violated, and very few of them were completely sure of their own being.

The Institute of Planetary Opinion published the first returns from an instant poll. It was a collective neurosis, a sudden surge in the death wish. Mass therapy and nationalization of schools of psychoanalysis were proposed.

A theologian replied: "Love of the flesh is death. Saint Paul saw that long before Freud, and he saw it better. By 'flesh' he meant all of man, including intelligence and the soul. And it is not that we love death *per se*. Quite the contrary. The flesh loves what it expects will deflect death. It is life as you lead it which leads to death and deserves it. We have simply reached Judgment Day. Your vitality will be judged as well as your mortality. For it does not come from us, but from the Other Side. There the future awaits us—the future we thought was only a retreat from the present. Here time finally affirms the moment that judges and ends *our* time, which was no more than our refusal of eternity. And history, complete in this affirmation, manifests itself on the Day of all days."

Even as he was speaking, a dawn glow appeared and grew around them. All things plunged back into their original amazement, all creatures were given up at once to the violence of the decisive act—we will finally see their justification, their being.

The instant was at hand when men saw that their efforts and cares were directed toward nothing, toward a painful Absence, while only Presence in all its splendor is terrible and difficult to tolerate; only love is almost tolerable, for it finds us unprepared. They had barricades only on the other side, the side facing this ill-framed world.

A new sun appeared. And those who saw it took on a new aspect. Their eyes grew strong, and they awaited an even brighter light. By degrees the Great Day burst upon them, ever vaster and whiter throughout the universe.

At first they felt embarrassed, clumsy, hardly knowing how to behave. And still the light grew. They were already falling, whole rows at a time, blinded and riveted where they stood by the certainty of bursting love. Some marched on, though, laughing joyfully at the dawn, moving on toward noon with the ease of those who are used to being at court.

Very few endured the last suns and the growth of the light to the limits of its perfection, where all that sees sheds light as well, where all eyes reflect what they receive, where the great day is everything in all.

The First Judgment was the Greeting.

Second Judgment, or Summons

This is the principle of the Second Judgment: Each man, pushed to the limit of his expression and forced to the extremity of his choice, cried out the "terms" of his life, spouted it all forth in that cry—a unique response to the eternal summons—the absolute value of his days and nights, his thoughts and his deeds, his knowledge, his refusals, his blindnesses, his affection. Thus was declared the incomparable quality of his sin, thus was measured the extent of existence of his inner being as he had freely shaped it in living.

Inspection of the reasons for survival and their introduction as exhibits for eternity took less time than one would think. Indeed, the procedure was quite simple.

"Bear witness," they said, "concerning your life. What is your truest desire?"

The wise replied, "No man truly has anything but what he can give away. Ask rather what I wish to die for."

And that was exactly what they did. Thus all became acquainted with death, but some were reborn in the heart of their greatest fear; others, in the comforting features of desire.

Most hesitated before the suddenly flagrant banality of their desires and at last murmured weakly, "You know better than I." Thanks to some sort of pity, they were reborn as happy plants. A man came, as sleepwalkers come, his body at peace, but his face horribly naked. He wanted an empty palace that would be proportionate to his sorrow. So he became a Wandering Jew, taking on the form of the joys he met, and his wish was granted. Another wanted to live fully in the bosom of perpetual poverty. He became a sunflower.

And who is this, who approaches with a partly opened umbrella under his arm and surly eyeglasses above a smile of fervent irony? What is he muttering under his straw hat?* He is saying that he wanted to live in this moment of choice a more violent life than he had ever dared imagine. For, he says, such a choice, he would grow immeasurably closer to the One who had chosen to create him.

We were all struck dizzy by his immoderate wish, but some sort of silence enveloped us and the lower reaches of heaven. From higher up, we could hear the ruling chorus of angelic laughter, solitary and purified. And we knew that man was very great.

Third Judgment, or Pardon

Everything has its place now, all flesh its time, and all spirit its wings. And each of us accedes to the fate he has made for himself, to perfect self-possession, to his hell or his heaven, in the consummation of all his being, to the unimagined pinnacle of desire satisfied for all eternity.

"But the Spirit and the Bride say: Come. And may the hearer say, Come! to him who carries with him the recompense of our works"—*it is in Him, not in our works.*

The work of the Pardon begins.

"And let him who thirsts come forth. Let him who wishes partake of the water of life, freely."

For now all has been paid for. All is freely given.

And that is when the mingled voices of the Just will proclaim the violent and blessed harmony of the sacrament of all Creation, the monumental end of the glory of the Omnipotent God—the Amen of Time kneeling and engulfed forever.

Water

or The Spirit of the Storm

1. The Spirit danced on the face of the waters, for the Storm had not yet penetrated the depths. When the Spirit grew calm, the waters died back, happy.

2. When the Spirit descended upon the waters and its dance was drowned beneath the sea, the Storm became the soul of the waters.

3. The seas brought to their surface the Ark of Peace; but those who still wanted to dance for the sake of dancing were drowned: They sought the dance in the depths where the Spirit, for the sake of peace, had once abandoned it. In great storms, they found death.

4. The seas, troubled by the Spirit, submerged the Psalmist. Pain had drowned him, and his salvation lies only in death by drowning. Bitterness accepted unto death purifies him and returns him to the Spirit.

5. The water of the Baptist is the mortal water of the Spirit, the dance of the Spirit in the souls of children, the mother water. And man drowns in it and dies of pain; he is drowned by bitterness, not by water. It is the taste of a new life.

6. "You are the salt of the earth," they were told. But the Spirit dances in salt waters. Contemplate the symbol of the Fish. He alone can live in the seas, in the bitterness and in the dance.

7. The seas are not for our thirsts, for the thirsty find only a desert there. It is like a fire. To die of thirst in the waters of bitterness, where drunkenness is impossible, and where the salt tastes of death, that is the very life of the Spirit, death of life, and life of the vast dance. Afterwards we must live on earth with its sharp salt.

8. For all those drowned in bitter water, where the Spirit dances in the deep waves, Christ has promised Living Water freely. Once the bitter has been accepted, death by water is the price of the Kingdom, a pure gift.

9. Thus for twice-born man, dead by water and the salt of the dance, but revived by the Living Water, there are no more tolls. The Spirit bears him upon the waters like a flight of doves.

Antaeus

or *The Earth*

Antaeus the giant, world champion, suffers from the strong man's obsession, which is the fear of not doing justice to one's strength all the time. Noblesse oblige, all or nothing. If he loses once, it's all over. He is never more worried than on the night before a championship fight, at the end of the most rigorous training. His manager has isolated him for months: no wine, no women, no lazy days, and no casual wandering. He has lived by the clock, down to the second, with nothing impure. And yet he feels impure and weak. Physically lightened by a strict diet, all his muscles moving freely and tensing instantly, his weight precise, and his vision clear, he nevertheless feels feverish. It is not eagerness to fight, but an obsessive need to give himself up to delirium and unchecked dissipation.

Because his manager knows these inclinations well, he tells reporters they are "neurotic tendencies due to our man's hypersensitivity," a pronouncement which has contributed more than a little to the champion's popularity. Today's fans adore heroes who are a little unstable. These weaknesses make them, in the current vernacular, more "human."

The fact is that until now, Antaeus, with a cunning that surpasses his muscular victories, has always managed to escape for a few hours on the eve of a key match. But the next day he shows up again, just before the fight, horrible to behold, his face spattered with mud, his clothes in shreds, his hands covered with scratches, and his nails broken. He seems exhausted, panting and sweating, throws himself into the fight, and wins.

(Below are a few excerpts from notes taken by the analyst who kindly took on his case, after the manager's repeated entreaties.)

"Oedipus complex: was forced to give up that idea after two years' hard work. Parents' life normal, even exemplary.* Patient's sex life normal, except for a few periods of prolonged abstinence coinciding with training periods. Slight dislike for giantesses to whom people introduce him. Typical nightmare: He is walking in an empty city . . . macadam and reinforced concrete phobia, metal structures phobia . . . fear of being out of his element.

"All of that would not have gotten me very far. But as sometimes happens, the patient himself finally gave me the key to his mystery.

"During one of our last sessions, I hazarded a courteous reference to the well-known legend about him. He flew into a terrible rage, broke the couch in two like a matchstick, shouting, 'It's just the opposite! Just the opposite!' 'The opposite of what?' I asked. 'The opposite of what they've been saying about me, the opposite of the encyclopedia, the opposite of you, your ideas —the opposite of everything!'

"I didn't argue with these last words. They offend my sense of logic, but I have some pretty expensive furniture. I even pretended to go along with the idea of "the opposite of everything."

During the next sessions, he expressed himself more calmly. For the sake of clarity, I deeply regret my patient's obviously deficient conceptual apparatus, but it is my duty to record or summarize his words (I did not get all of the slang) in the form in which, with some difficulty, he spoke them.

" 'Harry's trying to kill me. [Harry is his manager.] Don't want me to get drunk. Don't want me runnin' around. Don't want nothin'. Always clean is how he wants me. I get dirt on my hands, see, and they say I'm dirty. That makes me mad. I wash. With dirt, that's how I wash. . . . It's just the opposite. They say that's where I get my strength from. It ain't true. It don't come up to me outta the ground. It's the opposite. The dirt goes back into the earth. You gotta clean out your guts; it ain't soap and after-shave. When I get the humors, I feel weak. I'm all bloated. It gets on my nerves. The more he shuts me up in those pretty rooms, the worse I get. It can't get out no more, and it gets to me. It works up my blood. Humors, they say. Does anyone even know what humors are? I always get it in town. Once they're done washing me, massaging me, powdering me all over like a baby, there you are! The elevator, the marble, the cement, the asphalt, the car, and the dishes! All clean, all smooth, all polished —nothing to touch. You get it? All my dirtiness stays in my body. Won't come out of me. I start thinking I'm gonna lose. I say, "You ain't gonna make it this time. You're too nervous." Drives me crazy! But God loves me. I always get away. Harry wants to kill me. He runs from bar to bar. I take off for the countryside fast as I can. And there, Doctor, I let go! I roll on the ground and dig in the earth, run around naked, chew leaves, claw the trees, kiss the earth, sleep on the ground, and when I wake up covered with earth the next morning, I feel clean! The woods, the brush, the leaves, it's like women! My weakness goes into the ground during the night. See, it's just the opposite of what they say. Look at the dead and all their sicknesses—the earth sure makes you feel clean.' "

Fire

Sometimes, by the fireside, a long silence leads to another story, for it surrounds people with emptiness. Emptiness is insatiable.

Thus she started a story:

"The Indians acknowledged nothing but sleep, the deepest forgetfulness, when one exists by not existing. To enter that state, you had to throw yourself into the abyss. Anything that was only destruction was acknowledged.

"But soon they saw that people were beginning to doubt emptiness, the abyss, and destruction. Everyone could enter into them, but they could not really be reunited in forgetfulness. It was not the true beginning of all things.

"Then priests told them that they could acknowledge light, that light was like emptiness.

"Then other priests discovered that light means water, because water rejects bodies and will not have them. Water is emptiness. So water was acknowledged.

"And from the water came the Monster of the Water, insatiable, who wants to eat everything. That too was emptiness, so the Monster was acknowledged.

"And the Monster made them fear fire, the enemy of water, by telling them that Fire was the strongest of all, devouring all, wanting nothing to exist or appear. Wherever there was form, fire leaped upon it with its flames: It was the strongest form of nothingness.

"And prayer was invented, with chants, to tame flame and fire. Women threw themselves into the flame, because only destruction can feed or destroy destruction. They didn't need fire for heat or cooking in the tropics. Fire was only the guest who destroyed forests, people, and houses, once admitted."

We watched the fire in the hearth. I thought of love, insatiable as emptiness and fire, and I acknowledged love, the flame woman.

I thought of joy which makes us suffer and makes us alone. Of the West, which wants plenitude and creates emptiness, feeding monsters and fire despite itself. Of the mystics' path of negation, of these witnesses of the emptiness among us, the path which leads to the Beginning of all things, which is the true End.

Notes on the Unmapped Road

You ought to be as rational as possible, but no more. You will see just how far that goes, and then you will see better what goes further. Error does not show us the road. But let us try to think back to the question that we so often avoid by taking a mysterious detour. What is the destiny of one man, my destiny? Here the road begins.

You have a destiny if you are distinct.

As soon as he sees that he is set apart by fate, every man becomes superstitious; that is his unmapped road. The explorer travels far away to discover his own amulets. The pilot makes a secret mark on the propellor. Before H hour or while waiting for a lover, some ceremony will prepare you for the thread of opportunity or the cadence of grace. Risk and isolation return us to childhood, because they deliver us up to private magic.

To think or feel oneself unique is the most basic superstition. The others easily follow it, as the body follows the head at birth. For if I am unique, there is a road marked out for me alone. Only I can detect it as one writes a poem—or rather, as one meets a poem that he invents by picking up a wandering rhythm. From that moment I enter into the incomparable, where the trail is blazed by the footsteps that follow it. (If I take a known and safe road, no matter where I arrive, I will have lost myself on the way.)

In the insignificance of a life in which only money and war can draw a crowd, a superstitious man will simply be the one who does not despair of finding some sense behind the uniform absurdity he sees. He is the only one among us who has reason to be optimistic without being a fool.

If he settles for a probability which is strangely clear in his eyes, that is because it seems to deny the nothingness of the obvious roads, because it anticipates what will come, or because it is less probable than the others, and more of an apparition.

Some evenings, he comes slowly down his stairs, crosses the

threshold, pauses for a moment, and starts to walk along the road. His demeanor is unmistakable. It is the masterful caution of someone about to march the road to war. Red lights, green eyes, an averted profile at the intersection of two streets. It is New York, whose sum is 6 and its product 9—the demonic and the divine, for him—though it is really Sixth Avenue and Ninth Street. If he thinks about it, he is playing the game, in a meaningful and rhythmic way. He no longer sees the ladder, the black cat, the white horses, or the bearded priests. He does not expect any occult sayings, but awaits something that resembles nothing, which he will recognize at first sight: a chalk mark on the threshold of his life, a note that he alone can hear because it resolves his private dissonance and brings him into harmony with his destiny. Searching for what responds to him alone and reveals instantaneous peace, he follows the sound of that note the way an airplane follows a C-sharp through the night.

Let everyone, therefore, discover the symbols and the road that he alone can map out, so that he can draw closer to the mysteries all men share.

But this symbolic substance is curiously restricted, the numbers of useful symbols limited. Only a great genius could create a single new one. In games (the dreams of consciousness), and in dreams (the games of the unconscious), one can quickly draw up a list of these symbols. All are reduced to stock characters and geometric forms: kings and queens, castles and fortresses, soldiers or pawns; circles, squares, helixes, and crosses; Anima like a savage woman, desirable and elusive, and the Old Man who judges, both of them faceless. These forms and figures seem to be almost the only ones that can decode the messages sent by something above (or below) my watching self. Canals, locks, or tested signals stake out the unmapped road, the blossoms of that "rhetoric of dreams" which Jean-Paul was the first to name. They regulate the traffic between the obvious and the subterranean.

When I speak of dreams and games, I mean great dreams and true games. Of course for everyday use, as for anything derived from the dream that reflects it, any object would serve: an old twisted nail, a nickel statuette, a black pebble, a lost playing card stepped on by accident. But here we are touching on fetishism, which is merely a morbid obsession with the meaning of symbols.

When all closes in front of me, and nothing shows me how to act or escape from an impasse, I draw the cards and acknowledge with a wink my improvised superstitions. What am I doing, then, but rebuilding myself on my unconscious foundations, if reason hesitates or remains silent?

On the one hand, the symbols that I welcome are very likely to be in collusion with my secret need. It is that need, in fact, which selects them on the basis of a preliminary inclination, willingness, or vision. The symbols reveal my self to my eyes.

On the other hand, it may be that these symbols are steeped in the deep reality of myth, which regulates obvious dangers and permits me to recognize certain features and other manifestations of its structure.

Everyone acts thus, who when in doubt, turns to his tradition, to ancestral customs, to maxims—the registered symbols of the collective unconscious which replace reason when reason fails.

The superstitious man tests his destiny every day.

Then someone comes to him and says, "You remember only the lucky coincidences, premonitions, and providential forecasts. As the law of probability predicts, you may be lucky one time out of ten. You overlook all the times it fails. It fails at least nine times out of ten, like all your laboratory experiments. And like you, I remember only the tenth time, which gives me some direction. But the other nine have been neither futile nor mute. After all, they told me, 'You are not you, you are not here, you are no longer, you are not yet.' They brought me back to myself."

The superstitious man, if he is great, will go far. On the road of the incomparable, he may go to the very end of himself.

A common mistake: If chance does not exist, everything is determined. There is no alternative but to follow a rigid path drawn by destiny.

This mistake should make one blush.

Chance does not exist, but we are still free. I do not know who is making use of me, but the constraint, if there is one, is certainly not mechanical. A voice insists or ceases to insist; it speaks more or less clearly; doors close and open again; my hearing is more or less acute; I find or lose my bearings. It is an immense love affair! We are not drawn like filings to a magnet; we are loved by destiny. And sometimes destiny treats us indifferently, sometimes it wounds us, sometimes it oppresses us.

The rationalist pronounces it determinism. He sees a rail and thinks of regulation by an anonymous dictatorship.

I imagine an active and playful destiny.

Pause for a moment, please, before this truly dramatic innovation. What a blow to our philosophies! Name one that would recover from it. Just one!

One idea holds me back, probably more than I have ever admitted: the idea of universal instantaneous change that no one would suspect.

It is not on such a belief that wishes, incantations, magic, and prayer rest?

"To believe," said Kierkegaard, "that God is capable of everything at every moment, that is the health of faith."

Lovers are equally superstitious because every love is unique and must therefore invent symbols, signs, marks, and measures. Science stays silent or says, like everyone throughout the hundred thousand years that there have been men and love: It's skin deep. That's where we are.

One would get a bit further by calling it a question of stars.

The poet is equally superstitious because he feels at every moment the stealthy company of the same question: Does the poet follow his road or invent it? Does he invent it only by following wherever it leads, or does he follow it only by inventing whatever it becomes?

Does one *create* or *meet* a poem, a destiny, a love, a vocation?

"I never knew," admits the poet, "whether I invented a line or found it like a lost memory, like a dream that foundered which I dragged to the banks of consciousness by a wisp of hair, by the hand. . . . It resisted and for a moment drew me into its dawning death."

Poetry and superstition: They have the same laws, the same doubts, the same failures, and the same successes. And also the same—often vulgar—tricks. The poet believes in exactly 12 syllables. The superstitious man believes in the 21st of the month at precisely 7 o'clock. And one lovely night the perfect line arrives on 12 feet, and the woman is at the rendezvous.

(Repeat this to a jury. Try to reenact the experience, as their procedure demands. Nevertheless, it is true.)

There is good and bad superstition, just as there is good and bad poetry.

And let us add that the truly superstitious man scoffs at superstitions just as the true poet scoffs at poetic subjects and words, no more, no less. Both make fun of them and have fun with them.

Notes

Page xi. Jean-Paul Richter, 1763–1825, the great German romanticist.

Page 6. The painter is alluding to a conversation in which he and the husband agreed on the following point: Ethics and aesthetics are not two opposable realities. In their full meanings, these words are interchangeable. In both cases, one has to know "what is done." But does this propriety embrace *images* or *existences?*

Page 27. Corneille, *Cinna.*

Page 30. "Le soleil ni la mort ne se peuvent regarder en face" (de la Rochefoucauld, *Maximes*, 1665).

Page 35. Three Essays on the Theory of Sexuality. The definition of "normal" here is thus "adapted to the environment." Freud speaks of the truth of experience, and by virtue of this title, it has some value. But it is obvious that such a rule could lead to "totalitarian" conformity. One should accept a truth of this sort only by insisting on its opposite: "The abnormal" can create new sorts of social relations, or a new normality.

Page 35. In his story "The Shadow," Andersen tells how a philosopher "from the cold regions of the north," traveling in warm countries, loses his shadow because of a young woman he sees from his window. "In these warm climates," says Andersen, "things grow very quickly, and after a week he sees, much to his joy, that a new shadow has started to grow from his feet while he is walking in the sun." Here there is no morbid fascination, as with Schlemihl. Nor is the Devil the source of the adventure this time.

Page 36. According to Paracelsus, semen is distinguished from the *Liquor Vitae* "like the scum from the soup." Creativity is purified by getting rid of it. It thus appears that Freudianism is concerned only with the scum of the soup. Or is it called libido?

Page 38. This essay was a year old when I discovered in the *Notebooks* of Barrès (vol. 8, p. 86) two letters by a grandnephew of Chamisso's which seemed to invalidate my interpretation beforehand. Their author, a M. de Rubelles, considered—as did Barrès—that in *Schlemihl*, Chamisso "permits us to understand the tragic destiny of a man who is incomplete and without a country." Here are some curious memories of his granduncle: "He was, it seems, a bundle of nerves, exceedingly impressionable, with a core of somewhat permanent sadness, a perpetual description. *Peter Schlemihl* is certainly, if not an autobiography, at least a moral essay inspired by his own feelings. A state of the soul, we would call it today. The qualifying 'of the man who lost his shadow' was discovered by M. de Rubelles, who, seeing him in one of his habitual black moods, laughingly told him that he looked like a knight who had lost everything, even his own shadow. The phrase struck him and stayed with him." Besides the fact that this rationalistic interpretation (not entirely absurd) explains none of the story's peculiarities, one can think that Chamisso's state of the soul" played a more decisive role in this affair than did the gentleman's "might have been."

Page 60. Jean-Paul Richter, 1763–1825, the great German romanticist. In *Die Flegeljahre.*

Page 70. Søren Kierkegaard, as depicted in a caricature.

Page 73. Antaeus is the son of Poseidon and Earth. Since the separation of the waters, their arguments have been reduced to little spats. The relations between Earth and Fire are much more dramatic.

Colophon

This book is set in Palatino types, a letter designed by Hermann Zapf and named for the Italian Scribe. The version used here is the Linotype one. The book is printed directly from the type on Warren's Olde Style antique wove paper, and bound in cloth from the Columbia Mills. It was designed by Gary Gore.